Mediterranean Refresh Air Fryer Cookbook for Beginners

500-Day Mouth-Watering and Healthy Recipes to Fry, Roast, Bake, and Grill Most Wanted Family Meals

Kedry Yamos

Table of contents

Introduction

The Mediterranean Refresh Air Fryer is definitely for you. Especially Mediterranean diet, do you love fried food, but not the excess fat? Air fryers make it easy to satisfy taste buds while living with Mediterranean lifestyle. Learn to manage your diet and get great-tasting foods, too. An air fryer offers a healthy cooking option for Mediterranean dieters and is the perfect tool to cook a wide range of Mediterranean-friendly foods from vegetables to bean, fish to seafood, and even desserts. The Mediterranean Air Fryer Diet Cookbook will introduce you to over 500-day tasty and easy Mediterranean meals you can make with your air fryer.

Mediterranean foods are not only good for you but taste great too. The diet remains the best possible way to get healthy and rapidly lose weight. Mediterranean Refresh Air Fryer is so much more than just a healthy way to enjoy some crispy fried foods without worrying about getting fat. It is an appliance that can cook an incredible variety of dishes, including many that you probably never thought possible.

Chapter 1: The Basics of Mediterranean Diet

What Is the Mediterranean Diet?

The Mediterranean Sea is the sea that is fully bordered by landmass, the northern border formed by the southern European countries such as Turkey and Greece, and the southern border by the African countries like Egypt. The different countries' traditions, cuisines, and products have been thoroughly blended, giving rise to a unique culture that is also shown in their food. The diet of the inhabitants living in this unique culture is known as the Mediterranean diet.

This diet was made famous by research that was held in 1970 to study coronary heart disease. It showed that the people living in these regions have a low risk of developing heart diseases compared to other parts of the world. Thus, its importance was heightened across the globe. The diet mainly consists of different varieties of vegetables, fruits, beans, legumes, nuts, and oils. There is also an abundance of seafood in their cuisines. The diet consists of a significant amount of fats which is provided by the white meat and olive oil. Unlike the oils produced by animal fat, these oils contain healthy fat, which helps to lower body cholesterol and keep the body healthy.

Many of their traditional dishes are not only popular for their health benefits but also are known delicacies with their rich amount of fresh vegetables and fruits, and a variety of sea flavors. Dishes as Prosciutto shows great use of grains, while Tabbouleh's main ingredients are vegetables.

Benefits of the Mediterranean Diet

The advantages provided by the diet are not limited to, providing just a delicious meal. The extensive research done in the last 50 years showed that this diet had been linked to improving the lives of natives of these regions by safeguarding them from an array of diseases. It is the main reason why the Mediterranean diet has been trending. Multiple people from different backgrounds belong in this area, and the food brings all those different people together.

There are many ways that the diet increases the mortality of human life. The oils present in the dishes driven from white meat and plants lowers LDL content, which is linked to heart diseases and blood pressure. Herbs are used in high quantity which has different medicinal properties. The diet because of the low use of sugar and sugary substitutes it has reduces the chances of diabetes and glucose levels remains controlled. It also improves vision and brain function due to increased uptake of vegetables and fruits, which provides adequate levels of vitamins and minerals. Due to improved brain function, the chances of developing Alzheimer's disease is low. Eating fresh ingredients also reduces the probability of cancer development. It also lowers the risk of developing rheumatoid arthritis and bone disorders.

The western world has been gripped with obesity and its associated diseases. The diet also helps people to reduce their appetite and lose weight. This may be the main reason why the inhabitants of Mediterranean regions are healthier compared to other western countries such as the US.

How Do I Start a Mediterranean Diet?

Mediterranean diet can be accomplished by anyone. It doesn't put stress over your body or your mind but on the contrary, rejuvenates it. Unlike other diet practices, eating only a few ingredients will not be enough. A vast array of vegetables, fruits, and other products are a part of this diet.

Eating Plans

First, the diet consists of many types of oils, and these can be sourced from mainly olive oil. Therefore, replace all animal made oil products mainly with olive oil. Fish and other seafood are also a good source of fat. They are rich in Omega 3 fats, which is very healthy for the body.

Secondly, cut down red meat as much as possible. It can be consumed in low amounts, but mainly the protein consumed is in the form of seafood, grains, and beans. Red meat can be taken in the form of lamb, chicken, and turkey. Eggs and dairy products can also be used.

Thirdly, drink a good amount of water each day. Water is overlooked in many diets, but for a good lifestyle, water intake is essential. Replace all your beverages with water. It is important to hydrate yourself whenever thirsty.

Lifestyle

Lastly and most important is the fact that the diet also requires the Individual to follow a healthy routine. Sleep should not be compromised. Sleep is vital in maintaining a healthy body and brain function. Adequate sleep and completing one's sleep cycle should be a routine. Exercises are done daily. By doing daily physical activities, one's weight will be controlled, and the entire body will benefit and become stronger in the process. Most diets don't discuss the effect of the mind on the body. Stresses on the mind should be kept to a minimum. All this together will not only increase your health but also your brain.

Chapter 2: The Basics of Air Fryer

What is an Air Fryer?

With technology giving birth to different and unique inventions every day to satisfy the hunger of innovation in society, the modernization of the everyday kitchen is also seen. As time passes by, many new machines are introduced into the daily life of a common man. Among the many devices that have made life more comfortable with their usefulness and design, the Air Fryer is also an excellent tool which has many benefits.

An Air Fryer is a device that cooks food not by using oil but by heated air with no compromise on the texture and flavor of the dish. The Air Fryer is not only used for frying up food but can also be used for many other tasks such as grilling or baking. It ensures that the food is cooked evenly and thoroughly. Its design is such that it fits in a compact area and works via electricity.

It has many different parts:

1. The frying basket: it is a stainless steel basket in which the food is placed for cooking. This can be replaced by any other utensils, such as a pizza pan.
2. The timer: the timer is set accordingly; a red light indicates when the time has been finished.
3. The temperature controller: The temperature of the Air Fryer has a high range from 175 to 400F. Adjust the temp knob to achieve the desired temperature.
4. The air inlet/outlet: It is used to release the hot air and steam arising during the cooking process from the back of the device. It is, therefore, important that the device remains kept in a spacious area.

Advantages of Using an Air Fryer

With the demand rising of fat-free and healthy food, air fried food has also become a hot topic. With innovation striving to make every day more efficient, the air fryer has many benefits to improve daily lives. It has many advantages:

- **Multi-purpose**

It is not only a fryer but also a griller, a baker, or a pizza maker. Instead of purchasing tens of different devices, one can only buy an air fryer to fulfill the many requirements of one's kitchen.

- **Healthier Food**

With the use of hot air instead of oil to cook the food, the food cooked has a significant reduction in oil and fat content. Fat is related to increasing the risk of many diseases, such as heart disease, hypertension, and obesity. It does all this without hindering the flavors of the food being cooked. Because the fryer evenly distributes heat, the air fried food is as crispy as oil fried.

- **Reduces Time consumption**

Air fryer is set for a given time and cooks food at the provided temperature thoroughly. Usually, to get healthy cooked food, one must slave over a hot stove for some time but because of the air fryer, time can be saved.

- **Reduces Injury**

There are a lot of accidents involving the kitchen, either someone's finger is burned, or hot oil is splattered all over. The air fryer does not require oil or an open flame, so many injuries linked with it are not a worry.

- **Reheating**

Leftover food to be reheated can be easily done with the help of an air fryer. Usually, reheating food takes a lot of effort and time, but the air fryer does this job very efficiently.

- **Easy to Use**

Cooking is a complicated process requiring a lot of skills, but the air fryer makes cooking very easy. The ingredients need only to be put into the machine, and buttons need to be pushed. Anyone, even someone with no prior experience with cooking, can make great meals.

How to Start Cooking in An Air Fryer?

Firstly, the Air Fryer must be in a spacious place to allow heat to escape and prevent damage to its parts. It should be put on top of a heat resistance surface.

Secondly, pull out the frying basket gently from the machine. It is recommended to preheat the device for 5 minutes before using it. Simply set the desired temperature for 5 mins and then after the time is completed, pull out the basket.

Now place the food inside the container. Not more than ⅔ of the container should be filled. If required, the container can be greased with an oil spray to avoid sticking of the food. If fatty foods are placed, add a little bit of water so that the container remains clean.

Now place the container gently inside and close the lid. The electric cord should be connected, and the time and temperature should be set. Both indicators should be on until the frying is completed.

The food can be stirred flipped or shaken as per requirement.

For grilling, the food must be flipped at regular intervals until it gets a good color on both sides.

When finished, a sound will go off. Push the off button just once, then wait for 30 seconds for the device to completely turn off.

When done, serve the food in a serving dish and leave the basket out of the device for some time before putting it back in.

How to Clean and Maintain Your Air Fryer

Maintaining the Air Fryer

- When buying the Air Fryer, quality needs to be addressed before anything else. Don't give in to or purchase an Air Fryer on the bases of reviews or price. It should be bought from an established, and authentic source.
- Don't overfill the device; the fryer basket needs space. If it is overloaded, the food will not be properly cooked, and the taste and texture will be affected.
- Don't place the Air Fryer just anywhere. It needs to be placed in an area that will allow some space. It should always be put on top of a heat resistance surface
- Don't put the basket back in the Fryer without it cooling it down first. It should be cleaned and cool when reinserted.
- Don't follow the instructions of temperature or time given on packages or recipes for ovens or microwaves. Air Fryer is its device, which requires the settings to be adjusted.

Cleaning of the Air Fryer

The air fryer needs to be cleaned every month. If it is left without cleaning, it will start to give off a smell. If some food pieces are stuck in the heating outlet, black smoke will start to come out of the device when turned on.

When cleaning the device, it is important to keep in mind that no corrosive or strong chemicals should be used in cleaning. Also, hard and abrasive brushes are to be avoided. They can cause damage to the stainless steel of the basket, which will be irreversible.

Before cleaning the equipment, the device should be turned off and left to completely cooled down. Unplug the device and neatly place the cord to avoid hindrance.

Firstly, the basket needs to be clean thoroughly. Due to use, the basket will accumulate grease over it, and it will be difficult to remove. Use water and dishwashing liquid to clean the surface of the basket. If the stains are not easily removed, then leave the basket filled with water and dishwashing liquid for a certain amount of time. Then with a sponge clean the basket.

After washing, the basket needs to be rubbed and dried by a kitchen towel. Once thoroughly dried, the basket should be reinserted.

Chapter 3: Foods to Eat

Here's is what you can eat and add in your meals for the Mediterranean diet

Protein

Chicken, turkey, lamb, fish, seafood, and vegan alternates like tofu, tempeh, and seitan

Fats and Oil

Olive oil, coconut oil, avocado oil, grass-fed butter

Vegetables

All vegetables such as red onion, tomatoes, broccoli, cauliflower, Brussel sprouts, zucchini, bell peppers, artichokes, cucumber, eggplant, olives, potatoes, sweet potatoes, turnip, yams, greens like kale, spinach, collard, arugula, and all root vegetables

Fruits

All fruits like peach, apricot, apple, grapes, pear, watermelon, dates, cherries, all berries like blackberries, raspberries, strawberries, and blueberries

Nuts and Seeds

Walnuts, almonds, hazelnuts, peanuts, pistachios, cashews, and all unsweetened nuts

Grains

Beans, lentils, chickpeas, whole grains, steel-cut and old-fashioned oatmeal, quinoa, wheat, bulgur, farro, couscous, corn, brown rice, buckwheat, whole-wheat pasta, whole-grain crackers, all-bran cereals

Dairy

Eggs, yogurt, low-fat cheeses, low-fat milk, buttermilk, feta cheese, Brie cheese, and goat cheese

Sweeteners

Erythritol, swerve sweetener, stevia, honey

Sauces and Condiments

No-sugar tomato sauce, pesto, apple cider vinegar, balsamic vinegar, low-sodium soy sauce, tahini sauce, aioli, unsweetened BBQ sauce, unsweetened tomato ketchup, organic teriyaki sauce, hummus

Drinks

Unsweetened, tea, unsweetened coffee, water, red wine

Herbs and Spices

All organic herbs and spices

Chapter 4: Foods to Avoid

Skip the following foods on the Mediterranean diet

Protein

Red meat such as of beef and pork, bacon, processed meat

Fats and Oil

Trans fat, margarine, high-fat butter

Nuts and Seeds

Nut butters, sugar-coated nuts

Grains

Sugar-sweetened cereals, ready-made waffles, pancakes, crackers, snack foods

Dairy

Ice cream, sweetened yogurt, processed cheeses

Sweeteners

White sugar

Drinks

Processed fruit juices, sweetened coffee, sweetened tea, soda

Chapter 5: Breakfast and Brunch

Broccoli Frittata

Preparation time: 5 minutes
Cooking time: 17 minutes
Servings: 4

Ingredients:

- ½ cup chopped broccoli florets
- ½ teaspoon salt
- ½ cup chopped bell pepper
- ¼ teaspoon ground black pepper
- 2 tablespoons almond milk, unsweetened
- 3 eggs
- 2 tablespoons grated parmesan cheese

Method:

1. Switch on the air fryer, insert fryer basket, then shut with its lid, set the fryer at 350 degrees F, and preheat for 5 minutes.
2. Meanwhile, take a heatproof dish, grease it with oil and then place bell peppers and florets in it.
3. Open the fryer, arrange the dish in the air fryer basket, close with its lid and cook for 7 minutes.
4. In the meantime, take a medium bowl, crack the eggs in it, add salt, black pepper and milk and then whisk until blended.
5. When the vegetables have cooked, pour the egg mixture over the vegetables, sprinkle cheese on top and then continue cooking for 10 minutes.
6. When the air fryer beeps, open its lid, take out the dish, cut frittata into slices and then serve.

Nutrition Value:

- Calories: 171 Cal
- Fat: 20.6 g
- Carbs: 5.6 g
- Protein: 16 g
- Fiber: 1.1 g

Omelet

Preparation time: 5 minutes
Cooking time: 15 minutes
Servings: 1

Ingredients:

- 2 tablespoons chopped ham
- 2 tablespoons chopped red bell pepper
- 2 tablespoons sliced green onion
- 1 tablespoon chopped mushroom
- ¼ teaspoon salt
- 1 teaspoon breakfast seasoning
- 2 eggs
- ¼ cup coconut milk, unsweetened
- 2 tablespoons grated cheddar cheese
- 2 tablespoons grated mozzarella cheese

Method:

1. Switch on the air fryer, insert fryer baking pan, grease it with olive oil, then shut with its lid, set the fryer at 350 degrees F, and preheat for 5 minutes.
2. Meanwhile, place crack eggs in a bowl, whisk them until beaten, then add ham, pepper, onion, mushrooms, and salt and whisk until just mixed.
3. Open the fryer, pour in egg mixture, close with its lid and cook for 5 minutes.
4. Then sprinkle breakfast seasoning on top, scatter with cheeses and continue cooking for 5 minutes until cheese has melted and omelet has cooked.
5. When air fryer beeps, open its lid, take out the baking pan, slide omelet onto a serving plate and serve.

Nutrition Value:

- Calories: 350 Cal
- Fat: 16 g
- Carbs: 19 g
- Protein: 6 g
- Fiber: 2 g

Hash Browns

Preparation time: 30 minutes
Cooking time: 35 minutes |
Servings: 2

Ingredients:

- 1 small red onion, peeled, 1-inch sliced
- 1 1/2 pounds potatoes, peeled
- 1 medium red bell pepper, deseeded, 1-inch cubed
- 1 jalapeno, deseeded, cut into 1-inch rings
- 1/8 teaspoon salt
- 1/2 teaspoon ground cumin
- 1/8 teaspoon ground black pepper
- 1/2 teaspoon taco seasoning mix
- 1 1/2 tablespoon olive oil

Method:

1. Cut potatoes into 1-inch cubes, place them in a bowl, cover them with chilled water and let soak for 20 minutes.
2. Then switch on the air fryer, insert fryer basket, grease it with olive oil, then shut with its lid, set the fryer at 320 degrees F, and preheat for 5 minutes.
3. Meanwhile, drain the potatoes, pat dry with paper towels, place them in a bowl, drizzle with 1 tablespoon oil and toss until coated.
4. Open the fryer, add potatoes in it, close with its lid and cook for 18 minutes until nicely golden, shaking the basket every 5 minutes.
5. In the meantime, add onion, bell pepper, and jalapeno into the bowl that was used for potatoes, drizzle remaining oil over vegetables, season with salt, taco seasoning, black pepper, and cumin and toss until well coated.
6. When potatoes are done, add them to the bowl containing vegetable mixture and toss until mixed.
7. Return fryer basket into the air fryer, grease it with olive oil, then shut with its lid, set the fryer at 356 degrees F, and preheat for 5 minutes.
8. Then open the fryer, add the vegetable mixture in it, close with its lid and cook for 12 minutes until nicely golden and crispy, shaking the basket every 5 minutes.
9. When air fryer beeps, open its lid, transfer hash browns onto a serving plate and serve.

Nutrition Value:

- Calories: 186 Cal
- Fat: 4.3 g
- Carbs: 4 g
- Protein: 4 g
- Fiber: 4.8 g

Spinach Frittata

Preparation time: 5 minutes
Cooking time: 10 minutes
Servings: 4

Ingredients:

- 1 green onion, chopped
- ½ cup spinach leaves
- 2 tablespoons diced red bell pepper
- 1/8 teaspoon cayenne pepper
- 4 eggs
- ½ cup shredded cheese

Method:

1. Switch on the air fryer, insert fryer basket, grease it with non-stick cooking oil spray, then shut with its lid, set the fryer at 390 degrees F, and preheat for 5 minutes.
2. Meanwhile, take a large bowl, place all the ingredients in it, whisk until combined and then spoon the mixture into a heatproof dish greased with oil.
3. Open the fryer, arrange the prepared dish in the air fryer basket, close with its lid and cook for 10 minutes until thoroughly cooked.
4. Serve straight away.

Nutrition Value:

- Calories: 194 Cal
- Fat: 11.2 g
- Carbs: 4.1 g
- Protein: 12.8 g
- Fiber: 1.4 g

Frittata

Preparation time: 10 minutes
Cooking time: 14 minutes
Servings: 2

Ingredients:

- 1 ½ stick of Chinese waxed sausage, sliced lengthwise
- ¼ cup chopped kale
- ¼ cup baby spinach leaves
- 2 tablespoons corn
- 1 tablespoon chopped red onion
- 2 tablespoons peas
- 1 small green bell pepper, cored, julienne cut
- 1 medium carrot, peeled, julienne cut
- 1/8 teaspoon salt
- 1/8 teaspoon ground black pepper
- ¼ teaspoon olive oil
- 3 eggs

Method:

1. Switch on the air fryer, then shut with its lid, set the fryer at 350 degrees F, and preheat for 5 minutes.
2. Meanwhile, grease the air fryer baking pan, place sausage in it, add onion, stir until just mixed and spread evenly.
3. Open the fryer, insert baking pan in it, close with its lid and cook for 4 minutes.
4. Meanwhile, place the remaining ingredients in a bowl and whisk well until combined.
5. When air fryer beeps, open its lid, pour in the prepared batter, and continue cooking for 4 minutes.
6. Then increase air frying temperature to 390 degrees F and cook for 1 minute until the top of the frittata is nicely browned.
7. When air fryer beeps, open its lid, take out the baking pan, transfer frittata onto a serving plate, then cut it into slices and serve.

Nutrition Value:

- Calories: 290.5 Cal
- Fat: 19.7 g
- Carbs: 11 g
- Protein: 17.4 g
- Fiber: 2 g

Tofu Scramble

Preparation time: 10 minutes
Cooking time: 30 minutes
Servings: 3

Ingredients:

- 4 cups broccoli florets
- 1 block tofu, drained, pressed, 1-inch cubed
- 2 1/2 cups chopped red potato, 1-inch cubed
- 1/2 cup chopped red onion
- 1/2 teaspoon garlic powder
- 1/2 teaspoon onion powder
- 1 teaspoon ground turmeric
- 2 tablespoons soy sauce
- 2 tablespoons olive oil

Method:

1. Place tofu pieces in a bowl, add onion, onion powder, garlic powder, and turmeric, drizzle with 1 tablespoon olive oil and soy sauce, toss until well coated, and set aside to marinate until required.
2. Switch on the air fryer, insert fryer basket, grease it with olive oil, then shut with its lid, set the fryer at 400 degrees F, and preheat for 5 minutes.
3. Meanwhile, place potato pieces in a bowl, add remaining oil and toss until well coated.
4. Open the fryer, add potatoes pieces in it, close with its lid and cook for 15 minutes until nicely golden and crispy, shaking the basket every 5 minutes.
5. Then add marinated tofu pieces into the fryer basket, shake well, reserving the marinade, and continue cooking for 10 minutes at 370 degrees F, shaking the basket every 5 minutes.
6. In the meantime, add broccoli florets into the reserved marinade, toss until coated, and set aside until required.
7. After 10 minutes of frying, add broccoli into fryer basket, shake well to mix and cook for 5 minutes
8. When air fryer beeps, open its lid, transfer tofu, potatoes, and broccoli florets onto a serving plate and serve.

Nutrition Value:

- Calories: 276.3 Cal
- Fat: 12.3 g
- Carbs: 29 g
- Protein: 13.1 g
- Fiber: 5 g

Fried Guacamole

Preparation time: 6 hours and 15 minutes
Cooking time: 16 minutes
Servings: 10

Ingredients:

- 1/3 cup almond flour
- 1 egg

For Guacamole:

- 3 medium avocados, halved, pitted, peeled
- 1/3 cup chopped cilantro
- 1/3 cup chopped red onion
- ½ teaspoon ground black pepper

- 1 1/2 cups panko bread crumbs
- 1 egg white

- 2 teaspoons ground cumin
- 1 teaspoon of sea salt
- 8 tablespoons almond flour
- 1 lime, juiced

Method:

1. Prepare guacamole and for this, take a bowl, add all its ingredients in it except for flour and mash with a fork until well combined.
2. Gradually mix the flour until thick and brownie dough-like batter comes together and freeze for 1 to 2 hours until the mixture has hardened.
3. Meanwhile, take a baking sheet, and then line it with aluminum foil.
4. After 2 hours, use a spoon to scoop out guacamole, shape it into a ball, and then place onto the prepared baking sheet.
5. Prepare remaining guacamole balls in the same manner, cover the balls with aluminum foil, and then freeze for a minimum of 4 hours or overnight.
6. Then switch on the air fryer, insert fryer basket, grease it with olive oil, then shut with its lid, set the fryer at 220 degrees F, and preheat for 5 minutes.
7. In the meantime, crack the egg in a bowl, add egg white and whisk until combined.
8. Place bread crumbs in a shallow dish and then place almond flour in another shallow dish.
9. Working on one guacamole ball at a time, first spray the ball with oil, then coat with almond flour, dip into the egg mixture, then dredge with parmesan cheese and place the ball into heated fryer basket.
10. Fill the fryer basket with more guacamole balls in the single layer, spray with olive oil, close with its lid and cook for 8 minutes until nicely golden and crispy, shaking the basket halfway through.
11. When air fryer beeps, open its lid, transfer guacamole balls onto a serving plate, cook remaining guacamole balls in the same manner and serve.

Nutrition Value:

- Calories: 179 Cal
- Fat: 13 g
- Carbs: 14 g
- Protein: 6 g
- Fiber: 6 g

Breakfast Bombs

Preparation time: 10 minutes
Cooking time: 40 minutes
Servings: 4

Ingredients:

- 4 ounces whole-wheat pizza dough
- 3 slices of bacon, center-cut
- 1 tablespoon chopped fresh chives
- 3 large eggs, beaten
- 1-ounce cream cheese, softened, low-fat

Method:

1. Take a skillet pan, place it over medium heat, add bacon, and cook for 10 minutes until very crispy.
2. Then transfer bacon to a cutting board, let it cool for 3 minutes and then crumble it, set aside until required.
3. Pour beaten eggs into the skillet pan, stir and cook for 1 minute until eggs are almost set.
4. Transfer eggs into a bowl, add bacon, chives, and cream cheese and stir well until combined.
5. Switch on the air fryer, insert fryer basket, grease it with olive oil, then shut with its lid, set the fryer at 350 degrees F, and preheat for 5 minutes.
6. Meanwhile, divide pizza dough into four sections, roll each section into the 5-inch round crust, and then add one-fourth of the cooked egg mixture into the center of each crust.
7. Brush the edges of the crust with water and then form a purse by wrapping crust around the egg mixture.
8. Open the fryer, add crust in it in a single layer, then spray with olive oil, close with its lid and cook for 6 minutes until nicely golden brown.
9. When air fryer beeps, open its lid, transfer the breakfast bomb onto a serving plate and cook the remaining crust in the same manner.
10. Serve straight away.

Nutrition Value:

- Calories: 305 Cal
- Fat: 15 g
- Carbs: 26 g
- Protein: 19 g
- Fiber: 2 g

Crustless Mini Taco Quiche

Preparation time: 10 minutes
Cooking time: 28 minutes
Servings: 4

Ingredients:

- 1 medium green bell pepper, cored, diced
- ½ pound ground pork
- 1 small red onion, peeled, diced
- ½ pound ground beef
- 1 medium red bell pepper, cored, diced
- 1 teaspoon salt
- 2 tablespoons taco seasoning
- 1 teaspoon ground black pepper
- ¼ cup tomato salsa
- ¼ cup vegan heavy cream
- 4 eggs
- 1 cup shredded Mexican blend cheese

Method:

1. Take a medium skillet pan, place it over medium-high heat and when hot, add ground pork and beef.
2. Stir in salt and black pepper, and then cook the meat for 8 to 10 minutes until nicely browned.
3. Add onion and bell peppers, stir in taco seasoning and continue cooking the meat for 4 minutes until vegetables turn soft.
4. Meanwhile, take a large bowl, crack the eggs in it, add salsa, cream and cheese and then whisk until well combined.
5. Take four mini pie pans, grease them with oil, evenly fill the pans with the cooked meat mixture and then cover with the egg mixture.
6. Switch on the air fryer, insert fryer basket, then shut with its lid, set the fryer at 350 degrees F, and preheat for 5 minutes.
7. Open the fryer, arrange pie pans in the air fryer basket in a single layer, close with its lid and cook for 12 minutes until thoroughly cooked.
8. Serve straight away.

Nutrition Value:

- Calories: 100 Cal
- Fat: 100 g
- Carbs: 100 g
- Protein: 100 g
- Fiber: 100 g

French Toast Sticks

Preparation time: 10 minutes
Cooking time: 17 minutes
Servings: 2

Ingredients:

- 4 slices of almond bread
- 1/16 teaspoon salt
- 1/16 teaspoon ground cloves
- 1/16 teaspoon ground cinnamon
- 1 teaspoon Swerve icing sugar
- 1/16 teaspoon nutmeg
- 2 tablespoons unsalted butter, softened
- 2 eggs, lightly beaten

Method:

1. Crack the eggs in a bowl, whisk until beaten, then add salt, cloves, cinnamon, and nutmeg, and whisk until mixed.
2. Switch on the air fryer, insert fryer basket, grease it with olive oil, then shut with its lid, set the fryer at 350 degrees F, and preheat for 5 minutes.
3. Meanwhile, spread butter on both sides of bread slices, cut the slices into strips and then dredge into the egg batter.
4. Open the fryer, add bread strips in it in a single layer, spray with olive oil, close with its lid and cook for 6 minutes until nicely golden and crispy, flipping and spraying with oil halfway through.
5. When air fryer beeps, open its lid, transfer French toasts onto a serving plate and cook remaining bread strips in the same manner.
6. When done, sprinkle Swerve icing sugar on the French toasts and serve.

Nutrition Value:

- Calories: 178 Cal
- Fat: 15 g
- Carbs: 2 g
- Protein: 5 g
- Fiber: 0.5 g

Chapter 6: Poultry

Thai Chili Fried Chicken Wings

Preparation time: 40 minutes
Cooking time: 30 minutes
Servings: 2

Ingredients:

- 16 chicken wings
- 1/2 cup almond flour

For Thai Chili Marinade:

- 2 green onions, chopped
- 1 teaspoon grated ginger
- 1 ½ teaspoon minced garlic
- 1 teaspoon honey

- 2 ½ teaspoons chicken seasoning
- 1/4 cup buttermilk, low-fat

- 3 tablespoons soy sauce
- 1 teaspoon of rice wine vinegar
- 1 tablespoon Sriracha sauce
- 1 tablespoon sesame oil

Method:

1. Prepare the marinade, and for this, place all its ingredients in a blender and pulse for 1 minute until blended.
2. Pat dry chicken wings, place them in a large plastic bag, pour in the buttermilk, then add chicken seasoning, seal the bag, turn it upside down until chicken wings have coated, and then marinate in the refrigerator for a minimum of 30 minutes.
3. Once the chicken wings have marinated, switch on the air fryer, insert fryer basket, grease it with olive oil, then shut with its lid, set the fryer at 400 degrees F, and preheat for 5 minutes.
4. Meanwhile, place flour in another plastic bag, add marinated chicken wings in it, then seal the bag and shake until chicken wings have evenly coated with almond flour.
5. Open the fryer, stack chicken wings in it, spray with olive oil, close with its lid and cook for 15 minutes until nicely golden and thoroughly cooked, shaking the basket every 5 minutes and flipping the chicken wings halfway through.
6. When air fryer beeps, open its lid, take out the chicken wings and brush well with the prepared marinade.
7. Return chicken wings into the air fryer, shut with lid, and continue cooking for 7 to 10 minutes until glazed.
8. Serve straight away.

Nutrition Value:

- Calories: 202 Cal
- Fat: 11 g
- Carbs: 12 g

- Protein: 12 g
- Fiber: 2 g

Buffalo Chicken Wings

Preparation time: 5 minutes
Cooking time: 55 minutes
Servings: 4

Ingredients:

- 2 ½ pounds chicken wings

For Buffalo Sauce:

- 1 teaspoon garlic powder
- 1/4 teaspoon cayenne pepper
- 2 tablespoons apple cider vinegar

- 1 tablespoon olive oil

- 2/3 cup cayenne pepper sauce
- 1/2 cup unsalted butter, softened

Method:

1. Switch on the air fryer, insert fryer basket, grease it with olive oil, then shut with its lid, set the fryer at 360 degrees F, and preheat for 5 minutes.
2. Meanwhile, place chicken wings in a large bowl, add olive oil and massage it until evenly coated.
3. Open the fryer, add chicken wings in it in a single layer, close with its lid and cook for 25 minutes until nicely golden and thoroughly cooked, shaking the basket every 5 minutes and flipping the chicken wings halfway through.
4. Meanwhile, prepare buffalo sauce and for this, place a saucepan over medium heat, add all its ingredients in it, whisk well and cook for 3 to 5 minutes until sauce is warm through, set aside until required and keep it warm.
5. When air fryer beeps, open its lid, transfer fried chicken wings onto a plate, and cook remaining chicken wings in the same manner.
6. Add chicken wings into the sauce, toss until well coated and serve.

Nutrition Value:

- Calories: 481 Cal
- Fat: 41.5 g
- Carbs: 7.3 g

- Protein: 20.7 g
- Fiber: 0.1 g

Chicken Breast

Preparation time: 5 minutes
Cooking time: 15 minutes
Servings: 1

Ingredients:

- 7 ounces chicken breast, skinless
- 1 teaspoon chicken seasoning
- 2 teaspoons olive oil
- Mediterranean salad for serving

Method:

1. Switch on the air fryer, insert fryer basket, grease it with olive oil, then shut with its lid, set the fryer at 390 degrees F, and preheat for 5 minutes.
2. Meanwhile, coat chicken with oil and then season them with chicken seasoning on both sides.
3. Open the fryer, add chicken breasts in it, close with its lid and cook for 15 minutes until nicely golden and thoroughly cooked, shaking the basket every 5 minutes and flipping the chicken breast halfway through.
4. When air fryer beeps, open its lid, transfer chicken breast onto a cutting board, let it cool for 5 minutes and then cut it into slices.
5. Serve chicken with Mediterranean salad.

Nutrition Value:

- Calories: 262 Cal
- Fat: 6 g
- Carbs: 1 g
- Protein: 48 g
- Fiber: 0 g

Fennel Chicken

Preparation time: 40 minutes
Cooking time: 35 minutes
Servings: 4

Ingredients:

- 1 pound chicken thighs, boneless, skinless
- 1 large red onion, peeled, 1-1/2 inch sliced

- 2 teaspoons lemon juice
- 1/4 cup chopped cilantro

For Marinade:

- 2 teaspoons minced ginger
- 2 teaspoons minced garlic
- 1 teaspoon salt
- 1 teaspoon cayenne pepper
- 1 teaspoon turmeric

- 1 teaspoon smoked paprika
- 1 teaspoon garam masala
- 1 teaspoon ground fennel seeds
- 1 tablespoon olive oil

Method:

1. Prepare the marinade and for this, place all its ingredients in a large bowl and stir until combined.
2. Pierce chicken thighs with a fork, then add to marinade along with onion, toss until well coated and marinate for a minimum of 30 minutes in the refrigerator.
3. When chicken and vegetables have marinated, switch on the air fryer, insert fryer basket, grease it with olive oil, then shut with its lid, set the fryer at 360 degrees F, and preheat for 5 minutes.
4. Open the fryer, add chicken and onions in it, spray with olive oil, close with its lid and cook for 15 minutes until nicely golden and cooked, shaking the basket every 5 minutes.
5. When air fryer beeps, open its lid, transfer chicken and vegetables onto a serving plate, drizzle with lemon juice, sprinkle with cilantro, and serve.

Nutrition Value:

- Calories: 190 Cal
- Fat: 100 g
- Carbs: 100 g

- Protein: 100 g
- Fiber: 100 g

Crispy Chicken Dinner

Preparation time: 15 minutes
Cooking time: 16 minutes
Servings: 4

Ingredients:

- 4 chicken breasts, , each about 8 ounces, pounded
- ½ cup oats
- ¼ teaspoon salt and more as needed
- ¼ teaspoon ground black pepper and more as needed
- 1 cup buttermilk
- ¾ cup vegan cheese blend

Method:

1. Take a large bowl, place chicken breasts in it, pour in the milk, season with some salt and black pepper, toss until combined and then let the chicken marinate for 10 minutes.
2. Switch on the air fryer, insert fryer basket, grease it with non-stick cooking oil spray, then shut with its lid, set the fryer at 400 degrees F, and preheat for 5 minutes.
3. Meanwhile, take a shallow dish, place oats in it, and then stir in salt, black pepper, and cheese.
4. When the chicken has marinated, dredge it into oats mixture until well coated.
5. Open the fryer, arrange chicken breasts in the air fryer basket in a single layer, spray oil on the food, close with its lid and cook for 8 minutes until thoroughly cooked and golden brown, turning halfway.
6. Serve straight away.

Nutrition Value:

- Calories: 570 Cal
- Fat: 16 g
- Carbs: 49 g
- Protein: 55 g
- Fiber: 3 g

Mediterranean Breaded Chicken

Preparation time: 10 minutes
Cooking time: 30 minutes
Servings: 2

Ingredients:

- 2 large chicken breast, cut into nugget-style pieces
- ½ teaspoon salt
- 1 tablespoon dried thyme
- ½ teaspoon ground black pepper
- 3 ounces Tuscan herb granola
- 1 egg

Method:

1. Switch on the air fryer, insert fryer basket, grease it with olive oil, then shut with its lid, set the fryer at 350 degrees F, and preheat for 10 minutes.
2. Meanwhile, crack the egg in a bowl, whisk it until beaten and set aside until required.
3. Take granola in a plastic bag, seal it and then bash it with a rolling pin until the mixture resembles medium pieces.
4. Add salt, thyme, and black pepper into the granola, seal the bag and shake it until mixed.
5. Coat chicken pieces in the egg, then add them into the granola mixture, seal the bag and shake it until chicken pieces are evenly coated.
6. Open the fryer, add chicken nuggets in it in a single layer, spray with oil, close with its lid and cook for 20 minutes until nicely golden and crispy, shaking the basket every 5 minutes.
7. When air fryer beeps, open its lid, transfer chicken nuggets onto a serving plate and serve.

Nutrition Value:

- Calories: 453.5 Cal
- Fat: 17.1 g
- Carbs: 22.7 g
- Protein: 52.2 g
- Fiber: 2.7 g

Chicken Drumstick

Preparation time: 10 minutes
Cooking time: 25 minutes
Servings: 4

Ingredients:

- 2 1/2 pounds chicken drumsticks
- 1/4 cup coconut flour
- 1/2 teaspoon garlic powder
- 1/2 teaspoon sea salt
- 1 teaspoon smoked paprika
- 1/4 teaspoon ground black pepper
- 1/4 teaspoon dried thyme
- 2 large eggs
- 1 cup pork rinds

Method:

1. Place coconut flour in a shallow dish, add salt and black pepper and stir until mixed.
2. Crack eggs in another dish and then whisk until beaten.
3. Place pork rinds in another dish, add garlic, thyme, and pork rinds and stir until mixed.
4. Switch on the air fryer, insert fryer basket, grease it with olive oil, then shut with its lid, set the fryer at 400 degrees F, and preheat for 5 minutes.
5. Meanwhile, first coat chicken drumsticks into the coconut flour mixture, then dip into the eggs and dredge into pork rind mixture until evenly coated.
6. Open the fryer, add chicken drumsticks in it in a single layer, spray with olive oil, close with its lid and cook for 20 minutes until crispy and cooked, shaking the basket every 5 minutes.
7. When air fryer beeps, open its lid, transfer chicken drumsticks onto a serving plate, and cooking remaining drumsticks in the same manner.
8. Serve straight away.

Nutrition Value:

- Calories: 273 Cal
- Fat: 15 g
- Carbs: 3 g
- Protein: 28 g
- Fiber: 1 g

Caribbean Spiced Chicken

Preparation time: 10 minutes
Cooking time: 25 minutes
Servings: 8

Ingredients:

- 3 pounds chicken thigh, boneless, skinless
- 1 1/2 teaspoons ground ginger
- 1 tablespoon ground cinnamon
- 1 ½ teaspoon salt
- 1 tablespoon cayenne pepper
- 1 tablespoon ground coriander
- 1 teaspoon ground black pepper
- 1 1/2 teaspoons ground nutmeg
- 4 tablespoon olive oil

Method:

1. Pat dry chicken, then season with salt and black pepper on both sides and let it marinate for 30 minutes at room temperature.
2. Then switch on the air fryer, insert fryer basket, grease it with olive oil, then shut with its lid, set the fryer at 390 degrees F, and preheat for 5 minutes.
3. Meanwhile, brush chicken with oil and then season with remaining spices.
4. Open the fryer, add chicken thighs in it in a single layer, close with its lid and cook for 10 minutes until nicely golden and thoroughly cooked, shaking the basket every 5 minutes and turning the chicken halfway through.
5. When air fryer beeps, open its lid, transfer chicken onto a plate, wrap with aluminum foil to keep it warm, and cook the remaining chicken in the same manner.
6. Serve straight away.

Nutrition Value:

- Calories: 202 Cal
- Fat: 13.4 g
- Carbs: 1.7 g
- Protein: 25 g
- Fiber: 0.4 g

Buttermilk Chicken

Preparation time: 10 minutes
Cooking time: 15 minutes
Servings: 6

Ingredients:

- 1 ½ pound boneless, skinless chicken thighs
- 1 cup oats
- 1 cup almond flour
- ½ tablespoon ground black pepper
- 1 tablespoon seasoned salt
- 2 cups buttermilk

Method:

1. Take a large bowl, place chicken thighs in it, add buttermilk and then let the chicken rest in the refrigerator for a minimum of 4 hours.
2. Then switch on the air fryer, insert fryer basket, grease it with non-stick cooking oil spray, then shut with its lid, set the fryer at 380 degrees F, and preheat for 5 minutes.
3. Meanwhile, take a large plastic bag
4. place almond flour in it, add salt and black pepper and then add chicken thighs.
5. Seal the bag and then turn it upside down until chicken thighs are coated in flour.
6. Take a shallow dish and then place oats in it.
7. Working on chicken thigh at a time, dip into buttermilk and then dredge in oats until well coated.
8. Open the fryer, arrange prepared chicken thighs in the air fryer basket in a single layer, spray oil on the food, close with its lid and cook for 15 minutes until thoroughly cooked and golden brown, turning halfway.
9. Serve straight away.

Nutrition Value:

- Calories: 335 Cal
- Fat: 12.8 g
- Carbs: 33.2 g
- Protein: 24.5 g
- Fiber: 0.8 g

Tso's Chicken

Preparation time: 15 minutes
Cooking time: 45 minutes
Servings: 4

Ingredients:

- 1 pound chicken thighs, boneless, skinless, cut into1 to 1 1/4-inch chunk
- 2 tablespoons sliced green onion, divided
- 3 chiles de árbol, deseeded, chopped
- 1 tablespoon grated ginger
- 1 tablespoon minced garlic
- 1/4 teaspoon salt
- 1/4 teaspoon ground white pepper
- 1/3 cup and 2 teaspoons cornstarch, divided
- 2 teaspoons erythritol sweetener
- 2 teaspoons rice vinegar
- 1 1/2 tablespoons olive oil
- 1 teaspoon toasted sesame oil
- 2 tablespoons soy sauce
- 2 tablespoons ketchup
- 1 egg
- 7 tablespoons chicken broth
- 1/2 teaspoon toasted sesame seeds

Method:

1. Switch on the air fryer, insert fryer basket, grease it with olive oil, then shut with its lid, set the fryer at 400 degrees F, and preheat for 5 minutes.
2. Meanwhile, crack the egg in a large bowl and whisk until slightly beaten.
3. Cut chicken into 1 ¼-inch piece, add to the egg and toss until coated.
4. Place 1/3 cup cornstarch in a shallow dish, add salt and black pepper, stir well, then add chicken and stir until each chicken piece has coated.
5. Open the fryer, add chicken pieces in it in a single layer, spray them with oil, close with its lid and cook for 15 minutes until nicely golden and cooked, shaking the basket every 5 minutes and turning chicken pieces halfway through.
6. When air fryer beeps, open its lid, transfer chicken pieces onto a plate, and cook remaining chicken pieces in the same manner.
7. Meanwhile, place remaining cornstarch in a bowl, add sweetener, vinegar, soy sauce, ketchup, and chicken broth, whisk well, and set aside until required.
8. When all chicken pieces have cooked, place a large skillet pan over medium heat, add oil and when hot, add chilies and cook for 2 minutes until it starts to sizzles.
9. Add ginger and garlic, cook for 1 minute until fragrant, then pour in cornstarch mixture and stir well.
10. Switch heat to medium-high level, cook for 3 minutes until the sauce starts to bubble, then add chicken, stir until coated, and cook for 2 minutes until the sauce has thickened.

11. Remove skillet pan from the heat, add 1 tablespoon green onion, drizzle with sesame sauce, stir until mixed, and transfer chicken to a serving dish.
12. Sprinkle with sesame seeds, garnish with remaining green onion and serve.

Nutrition Value:

- Calories: 302 Cal
- Fat: 13 g
- Carbs: 18 g
- Protein: 26 g
- Fiber: 0 g

Chapter 7: Appetizers and Siders

Cauliflower

Preparation time: 5 minutes
Cooking time: 20 minutes
Servings: 5

Ingredients:

- 16 ounces cauliflower, cut into florets
- 2/3 teaspoon salt
- ½ teaspoon ground black pepper
- 2 teaspoons olive oil
- 1 tablespoon potato starch

Method:

1. Switch on the air fryer, insert fryer basket, grease it with olive oil, then shut with its lid, set the fryer at 400 degrees F, and preheat for 5 minutes.
2. Meanwhile, place cauliflower florets in a bowl, add remaining ingredients and toss until well coated.
3. Open the fryer, add cauliflower florets in it, close with its lid and cook for 15 minutes until nicely golden and crispy, shaking the basket every 5 minutes.
4. When air fryer beeps, open its lid, transfer cauliflower florets onto a serving plate and serve.

Nutrition Value:

- Calories: 36 Cal
- Fat: 1 g
- Carbs: 5 g
- Protein: 1 g
- Fiber: 1 g

Mac and Cheese

Preparation time: 10 minutes
Cooking time: 30 minutes
Servings: 2

Ingredients:

- 1 cup elbow macaroni, whole-wheat
- 1/2 cup broccoli florets
- ¼ teaspoon ground black pepper
- 1/3 teaspoon salt
- 1 1/2 cup grated cheddar cheese
- 1 tablespoon grated parmesan cheese
- 1/2 cup almond milk, warmed

Method:

1. Take a pot half full of water, place it over medium-high heat, bring it to boil, then add macaroni and broccoli and cook for 10 minutes until tender.
2. When done, drain macaroni and vegetables, transfer them in a bowl, pour in milk, add cheddar cheese, season with black pepper and salt, and stir until well mixed.
3. Switch on the air fryer, insert fryer basket, then shut with its lid, set the fryer at 350 degrees F, and preheat for 5 minutes.
4. Meanwhile, place mac and cheese mixture in a heatproof baking dish that fits into the air fryer and sprinkle parmesan cheese on top.
5. Open the fryer, place baking dish in it, close with its lid and cook for 15 minutes until pasta is bubbling.
6. When air fryer beeps, open its lid, take out the baking dish, let the pasta sit for 10 minutes, and then serve.

Nutrition Value:

- Calories: 320 Cal
- Fat: 17 g
- Carbs: 29 g
- Protein: 15 g
- Fiber: 2.8 g

Sweet Potato Cauliflower Patties

Preparation time: 15 minutes
Cooking time: 52 minutes
Servings: 10

Ingredients:

- 1 large sweet potato, peeled, diced
- 2 cup cauliflower florets
- 1 green onion, chopped
- 1 cup cilantro
- 1 teaspoon minced garlic
- 1/4 teaspoon salt
- 1/4 teaspoon ground black pepper
- 2 tablespoons ranch seasoning mix
- 2 tablespoons arrowroot starch
- 1/2 teaspoon red chili powder
- 1/4 cup ground flaxseed
- 1/4 teaspoon cumin
- 1/4 cup sunflower seeds

Method:

1. Place sweet potato pieces in a food processor and pulse until coarsely chopped.
2. Then add cauliflower florets along with garlic and onion and pulse again until combined.
3. Add remaining, pulse for 1 minute until thick batter comes together, then shape the batter into 8 to 10 patties and freeze them for 10 minutes.
4. Switch on the air fryer, insert fryer basket, grease it with olive oil, then shut with its lid, set the fryer at 370 degrees F, and preheat for 5 minutes.
5. Open the fryer, add prepared patties in it in a single layer, spray them with oil, close with its lid, and cook for 18 minutes until nicely golden and crispy, turning the patties halfway through.
6. When air fryer beeps, open its lid, transfer patties onto a serving plate, keep them warm and cook remaining patties in the same manner.
7. Serve straight away.

Nutrition Value:

- Calories: 85 Cal
- Fat: 3 g
- Carbs: 9 g
- Protein: 2.7 g
- Fiber: 3.5 g

Cauliflower Fritters

Preparation time: 10 minutes
Cooking time: 25 minutes
Servings: 4

Ingredients:

- ¼ of large cauliflower florets, chopped
- ½ cup coconut flour
- 1 ½ tablespoon chopped mint
- ½ cup buttermilk
- 3.5 ounces crumbled feta cheese
- 1 egg
- 3 tablespoons olive oil

Method:

1. Switch on the air fryer, insert fryer basket, grease it with non-stick cooking oil spray, then shut with its lid, set the fryer at 400 degrees F, and preheat for 5 minutes.
2. Meanwhile, take a large bowl, place cauliflower florets, add salt, black pepper and 1 ½ tablespoon and then toss until coated.
3. Open the fryer, place the cauliflower florets in the air fryer basket, close with its lid and cook for 15 minutes until thoroughly cooked, turning halfway.
4. Take a large bowl, crack the egg in it, whisk in flour and then whisk in milk until thick batter comes together.
5. Add cheese and mint, add cooked cauliflower and remaining oil and then stir until well combined.
6. Spoon the cauliflower mixture in the air fryer basket in a single layer, close with its lid and cook for 10 minutes until thoroughly cooked and golden brown, turning halfway.
7. Serve straight away.

Nutrition Value:

- Calories: 263 Cal
- Fat: 18 g
- Carbs: 17 g
- Protein: 9 g
- Fiber: 2 g

Seasoned Rutabaga Fries

Preparation time: 5 minutes
Cooking time: 15 minutes
Servings: 4

Ingredients:

- 1 rutabaga, peeled, cut into 1/2-inch wedges
- ¼ teaspoon garlic powder
- ½ teaspoon onion powder
- ½ teaspoon salt
- 1 teaspoon paprika
- ¼ teaspoon ground black pepper
- ½ teaspoon dried parsley
- 1 tablespoon olive oil

Method:

1. Switch on the air fryer, insert fryer basket, grease it with non-stick cooking oil spray, then shut with its lid, set the fryer at 400 degrees F, and preheat for 5 minutes.
2. Meanwhile, take a large bowl, place rutabaga wedges in it, add remaining ingredients and then toss until coated.
3. Open the fryer, arrange rutabaga wedges in the air fryer basket in a single layer, close with its lid and cook for 15 minutes until thoroughly cooked and golden brown, turning halfway.
4. Serve straight away.

Nutrition Value:

- Calories: 70 Cal
- Fat: 4 g
- Carbs: 9 g
- Protein: 1 g
- Fiber: 2 g

Patatas Bravas

Preparation time: 25 minutes
Cooking time: 20 minutes
Servings: 4

Ingredients:

- 12 ounces red potato, cut into 1-inch chunks
- 1/2 teaspoon ground black pepper
- 1/2 teaspoon sea salt
- 1 teaspoon garlic powder
- 1/2 teaspoon cayenne pepper
- 1 tablespoon smoked paprika
- 1 tablespoon coconut oil
- ¼ teaspoon dried chives
- Garlic aioli for serving

Method:

1. Take a pot, place it half-full of water over medium heat, bring the water to boil, add potato pieces, and cook for 6 minutes.
2. Then drain the potatoes, pat them dry, cool for 15 minutes and add them into a large bowl.
3. Add garlic into the potatoes, season with 1/8 teaspoon each of salt and black pepper, drizzle with oil and toss until coated.
4. Switch on the air fryer, insert fryer basket, grease it with olive oil, then shut with its lid, set the fryer at 390 degrees F, and preheat for 5 minutes.
5. Open the fryer, add potatoes in it in a single layer, spray them with olive oil, close with its lid and cook for 15 minutes until nicely golden and crispy, shaking the basket halfway through.
6. When air fryer beeps, open its lid, transfer potatoes to a bowl, add remaining ingredients, toss until coated, and serve them with garlic aioli.

Nutrition Value:

- Calories: 97 Cal
- Fat: 4 g
- Carbs: 15 g
- Protein: 1 g
- Fiber: 1 g

Onion Rings

Preparation time: 10 minutes
Cooking time: 22 minutes
Servings: 4

Ingredients:

- 1 large white onion, peeled, sliced into ½-inch thick rings
- 2/3 cup pork rinds
- 3 tablespoons coconut flour
- 3 tablespoons almond flour
- 1/2 teaspoon garlic powder
- 1/4 teaspoon sea salt
- 1/2 teaspoon paprika
- 2 eggs

Method:

1. Take a shallow dish, place coconut flour in it, add salt, stir until mixed and set aside until required.
2. Crack eggs in a bowl, whisk until combined, and set aside until required.
3. Place pork rinds in another shallow dish, add almond flour in it, season with garlic powder and paprika, and stir until mixed.
4. Switch on the air fryer, insert fryer basket, grease it with olive oil, then shut with its lid, set the fryer at 400 degrees F, and preheat for 5 minutes.
5. Meanwhile, prepare onion rings and for this, dredge them in coconut flour, dip them into beaten eggs and then coat with pork rind mixture.
6. Open the fryer, add onion rings in it in a single layer, spray olive oil, close with its lid and cook for 16 minutes until nicely golden and crispy, shaking the basket every 5 minutes.
7. When air fryer beeps, open its lid, transfer onion rings onto a serving plate, keep them warm and cook remaining onion rings in the same manner.
8. Serve straight away.

Nutrition Value:

- Calories: 135 Cal
- Fat: 7 g
- Carbs: 8 g
- Protein: 8 g
- Fiber: 3 g

Whole-Wheat Pizzas

Preparation time: 10 minutes
Cooking time: 25 minutes
Servings: 2

Ingredients:

- 2 whole-wheat pita rounds
- 1 small tomato, cut into eight slices
- ½ teaspoon minced garlic
- 1 cup baby spinach leaves
- 1/4 cup marinara sauce
- 1/4 cup shredded mozzarella cheese
- 1 tablespoon grated parmesan cheese

Method:

1. Switch on the air fryer, insert fryer basket, grease it with olive oil, then shut with its lid, set the fryer at 350 degrees F, and preheat for 10 minutes.
2. Meanwhile, prepare pizzas and for this, spread 1 tablespoon of marinara sauce on one side of each pita bread, then evenly top with spinach and tomatoes, and then sprinkle with garlic and cheeses.
3. Open the fryer, add one pizza in it, close with its lid and cook for 5 minutes until nicely golden and crispy.
4. When air fryer beeps, open its lid, transfer the pizza onto a serving plate, keep it warm, and cook remaining pizza in the same manner.
5. Serve straight away.

Nutrition Value:

- Calories: 229 Cal
- Fat: 5 g
- Carbs: 37 g
- Protein: 11 g
- Fiber: 5 g

Quiche

Preparation time: 5 minutes
Cooking time: 10 minutes
Servings: 1

Ingredients:

- 4 florets of broccoli
- 1 tablespoon vegan cheddar cheese
- 4 tablespoons vegan heavy cream
- 1 egg

Method:

1. Switch on the air fryer, insert fryer basket, then shut with its lid, set the fryer at 325 degrees F, and preheat for 5 minutes.
2. Meanwhile, take a 5-inch heat-proof quiche dish, grease it with oil, crack the egg in it and then whisk in cream.
3. Scatter broccoli florets on top of the mixture and then sprinkle with cheese.
4. Open the fryer, place the quiche dish in the air fryer basket, close with its lid and cook for 10 minutes until thoroughly cooked, turning halfway.
5. Serve straight away.

Nutrition Value:

- Calories: 656 Cal
- Fat: 58 g
- Carbs: 18 g
- Protein: 21 g
- Fiber: 6 g

Spicy Chicken Thighs

Preparation time: 10 minutes
Cooking time: 45 minutes
Servings: 4

Ingredients:

- 2 pounds chicken thighs, bone-in, skin-on
- 2 tablespoons sliced green onions, for garnish
- 1 teaspoon toasted sesame seeds, for garnish

For the Marinade:

- 1 teaspoon minced garlic
- 2 teaspoons grated ginger
- 2 tablespoons honey
- 1/3 cup soy sauce
- 1/4 cup olive oil
- 2 tablespoons chili garlic sauce
- 1 lime, juiced

Method:

1. Prepare the marinade and for this, place all its ingredients in a bowl and stir until combined.
2. Reserve half of the marinade, then pour remaining marinade in a bowl, add chicken thighs in it, toss until well coated and marinate in the refrigerator for 30 minutes.
3. Then switch on the air fryer, insert fryer basket, grease it with olive oil, then shut with its lid, set the fryer at 400 degrees F, and preheat for 5 minutes.
4. Open the fryer, add chicken thighs in it in a single layer, close with its lid and cook for 20 minutes until nicely golden and crispy, turning chicken thighs halfway through.
5. Meanwhile, pour remaining marinade in a saucepan, place it over medium heat, bring it to boil, and cook for 5 minutes until slightly thick, set aside until required.
6. When air fryer beeps, open its lid, transfer chicken thighs onto a serving plate, keep them warm and cook remaining chicken thighs in the same manner.
7. When done, brush chicken thighs generously with prepared sauce, sprinkle with green onion and sesame seeds, and serve.

Nutrition Value:

- Calories: 287 Cal
- Fat: 18.8 g
- Carbs: 3.6 g
- Protein: 26.5 g
- Fiber: 0.5 g

Chapter 8: Beef, Pork, and Lamb

Italian-Style Meatballs

Preparation time: 15 minutes
Cooking time: 25 minutes
Servings: 4

Ingredients:

- 2/3 pound ground beef
- 2 tablespoons minced shallots
- 1/3 pound turkey sausage
- 1 tablespoon minced garlic
- 1/4 cup chopped parsley
- 1 tablespoon Dijon mustard
- 1/2 teaspoon salt
- 1 tablespoon chopped thyme
- 1 tablespoon chopped rosemary
- 2 tablespoons olive oil
- 1 egg, beaten
- 1/4 cup whole-wheat panko crumbs
- 2 tablespoons almond milk
- Zucchini noodles for serving

Method:

1. Place panko crumbs in a bowl, add milk, stir and let it stand for 5 minutes.
2. Meanwhile, take a skillet pan, place it over medium-high heat, add oil and when hot, add shallots and cook for 2 minutes until softened.
3. Then add minced garlic, cook for 1 minute until fragrant, and then remove the pan from heat.
4. Add shallot mixture in a large bowl, pour in milk mixture along with sausage, beef, salt, thyme, rosemary, mustard, and parsley and stir until combined.
5. Switch on the air fryer, insert fryer basket, grease it with olive oil, then shut with its lid, set the fryer at 400 degrees F, and preheat for 5 minutes.
6. Meanwhile, prepare meatballs and for this, shape the beef mixture into 1 ½ inch meatballs.
7. Open the fryer, add meatballs in it in a single layer, spray them with olive oil, close with its lid and cook for 10 minutes until nicely golden and cooked through, shaking the basket every 5 minutes and turning meatballs halfway through.
8. When air fryer beeps, open its lid, transfer meatballs onto a serving plate, keep them warm and cook remaining meatballs in the same manner.
9. Serve meatballs with zucchini noodles.

Nutrition Value:

- Calories: 122 Cal
- Fat: 8 g
- Carbs: 0 g
- Protein: 10 g
- Fiber: 0 g

Super Quick Pork Chops

Preparation time: 10 minutes
Cooking time: 12 minutes
Servings: 3

Ingredients:

- 3 pork loin chops, each about 6 ounces
- 1 teaspoon minced garlic
- 1 teaspoon salt
- 1 tablespoon minced rosemary
- 1 teaspoon ground black pepper
- 4 ounces coconut butter, melted

Method:

1. Switch on the air fryer, insert fryer basket, grease it with non-stick cooking oil spray, then shut with its lid, set the fryer at 375 degrees F, and preheat for 5 minutes.
2. Meanwhile, take a small bowl, place garlic in it, add rosemary and butter and then stir until combined.
3. Season the pork chops with salt and black pepper and then drizzle with the rosemary-butter mixture until coated.
4. Open the fryer, arrange the prepared pork chops in the air fryer basket in a single layer, close with its lid and cook for 12 minutes until thoroughly cooked and golden brown, turning halfway.
5. When done, let the pork chops rest for 10 minutes and then serve.

Nutrition Value:

- Calories: 100 Cal
- Fat: 100 g
- Carbs: 100 g
- Protein: 100 g
- Fiber: 100 g

Spicy Lamb Steak

Preparation time: 40 minutes
Cooking time: 35 minutes
Servings: 4

Ingredients:

- 1 pound lamb sirloin steaks, boneless
- 4 slices of ginger
- 1/2 of a white onion
- 5 cloves of garlic, peeled
- 1 teaspoon ground fennel
- 1 teaspoon salt
- 1/2 teaspoon ground cardamom
- 1 teaspoon cayenne pepper
- 1 teaspoon garam masala
- 1 teaspoon ground cinnamon

Method:

1. Place all the ingredients in a blender, except for lamb, and pulse for 4 minutes until blended.
2. Place lamb chops in a bowl, make cuts in it with a knife, add marinade, toss until well coated and marinate for a minimum for 30 minutes.
3. Then switch on the air fryer, insert fryer basket, grease it with olive oil, then shut with its lid, set the fryer at 330 degrees F, and preheat for 5 minutes.
4. Open the fryer, add lamb steaks in it in a single layer, spray them with oil, close with its lid and cook for 15 minutes until nicely golden and cooked through, shaking the basket every 5 minutes, flipping halfway through.
5. When air fryer beeps, open its lid, transfer lamb steaks onto a serving plate, keep it warm and cook remaining steaks in the same manner.
6. Serve straight away.

Nutrition Value:

- Calories: 182 Cal
- Fat: 7 g
- Carbs: 3 g
- Protein: 24 g
- Fiber: 1 g

Steak Bites and Mushrooms

Preparation time: 5 minutes
Cooking time: 23 minutes
Servings: 4

Ingredients:

- 1 pound steaks, 1-inch cubed
- 8 ounces mushrooms, halved
- ¼ teaspoon ground black pepper
- 1/2 teaspoon garlic powder
- ¾ teaspoon salt
- 1 teaspoon Worcestershire sauce
- 2 tablespoons unsalted butter, melted
- 1 tablespoon minced parsley

Method:

1. Switch on the air fryer, insert fryer basket, grease it with olive oil, then shut with its lid, set the fryer at 400 degrees F, and preheat for 5 minutes.
2. Meanwhile, place steak cubes in a bowl, add mushrooms and stir until just mixed.
3. Drizzle with butter, season with garlic powder, black pepper, salt, and Worcestershire sauce and toss until well coated.
4. Open the fryer, add steaks and mushrooms in it, spread them evenly, close with its lid, and cook for 18 minutes until nicely golden and cooked, shaking and the basket and turning steaks every 5 minutes.
5. When air fryer beeps, open its lid, transfer steaks and mushrooms onto a serving plate and serve.

Nutrition Value:

- Calories: 330 Cal
- Fat: 21 g
- Carbs: 3 g
- Protein: 32 g
- Fiber: 1 g

Pork Chops with Brussels Sprouts

Preparation time: 5 minutes
Cooking time: 30 minutes
Servings: 1

Ingredients:

- 1 pork chop, bone-in, center-cut, about 8 ounces
- 6 ounces Brussels sprouts, cut into quarters
- 1/8 teaspoon salt
- 1 teaspoon agave syrup
- ½ teaspoon ground black pepper, divided
- 1 teaspoon mustard paste
- 1 teaspoon olive oil

Method:

1. Switch on the air fryer, insert fryer basket, grease it with non-stick cooking oil spray, then shut with its lid, set the fryer at 400 degrees F, and preheat for 5 minutes.
2. Meanwhile, rub the pork chop with oil and then season with salt and ¼ teaspoon black pepper.
3. Take a medium bowl, place remaining ingredients in it, add Brussels sprouts and then toss until coated.
4. Open the fryer, arrange pork chops and Brussels sprouts in the air fryer basket, close with its lid and cook for 13 minutes until thoroughly cooked and golden brown, turning halfway.
5. Serve straight away.

Nutrition Value:

- Calories: 337 Cal
- Fat: 11 g
- Carbs: 21 g
- Protein: 40 g
- Fiber: 10 g

Steak Nuggets

Preparation time: 40 minutes
Cooking time: 15 minutes
Servings: 4

Ingredients:

- 1 pound beef steak, cut into chunks
- 1 large egg

For Breading:

- 1/2 teaspoon seasoned salt
- 1/2 cup pork panko
- 1/2 cup grated parmesan cheese

For Chipotle Ranch Dip:

- 1/4 of a medium lime, juiced
- 1/2 teaspoon ranch dressing and dip mix
- 1 teaspoon chipotle paste
- 1/4 cup mayonnaise
- 1/4 cup sour cream

Method:

1. Prepare the ranch dip and for this, place all its ingredients in a bowl and whisk well until mixed; reserve its 1 teaspoon and refrigerate until required.
2. Prepare breading and for this, place all its ingredients in a shallow dish and stir until mixed.
3. Crack the egg in a bowl and then whisk well until blended.
4. Prepare nuggets and for this, dip steak pieces into the egg, then dredge into the breading until coated, arrange them on a sheet pan lined with baking paper and freeze for 30 minutes.
5. Then switch on the air fryer, insert fryer basket, grease it with olive oil, then shut with its lid, set the fryer at 325 degrees F, and preheat for 5 minutes.
6. Open the fryer, add steak nuggets in it in a single layer, spray with olive oil, close with its lid and cook for 3 minutes until nicely golden and cooked.
7. When air fryer beeps, open its lid, transfer nuggets onto a serving plate, keep warm and cook remaining nuggets in the same manner.
8. Serve nuggets with ranch dip.

Nutrition Value:

- Calories: 350 Cal
- Fat: 20 g
- Carbs: 1 g
- Protein: 40 g
- Fiber: 0 g

Glazed Pork Tenderloin

Preparation time: 10 minutes
Cooking time: 20 minutes
Servings: 4

Ingredients:

- 1.5-pound pork tenderloin, fat trimmed
- 2 cloves of garlic, peeled, sliced
- 1 teaspoon dried rosemary
- ¼ teaspoon salt
- 3 tablespoons coconut sugar
- ⅛ teaspoon ground black pepper
- 1 teaspoon Italian seasoning
- ¼ cup yellow mustard

Method:

1. Prepare the pork tenderloin and for this, make some slits in it and then stuff with garlic.
2. Take a small bowl, place all the seasonings and mustard in it and then stir until combined.
3. Rub the prepared spice mix all over the pork and then let it marinate for a minimum of 2 hours in the refrigerator.
4. When ready to cook, switch on the air fryer, insert the fryer basket, grease it with non-stick cooking oil spray, then shut with its lid, set the fryer at 400 degrees F, and preheat for 5 minutes.
5. Open the fryer, arrange the marinated pork tenderloin in the air fryer basket, spray oil on the food, close with its lid and cook for 20 minutes until thoroughly cooked, turning halfway.
6. When done, let the pork tenderloin rest for 5 minutes, cut it into slices and then serve.

Nutrition Value:

- Calories: 390 Cal
- Fat: 11 g
- Carbs: 11 g
- Protein: 59 g
- Fiber: 1 g

Meatloaf Sliders

Preparation time: 10 minutes
Cooking time: 30 minutes
Servings: 8

Ingredients:

- 1 pound ground beef
- ½ cup almond flour
- ¼ cup chopped red onion
- ¼ cup coconut flour
- 1 teaspoon minced garlic
- 1 teaspoon Italian seasoning
- ½ teaspoon ground black pepper
- ½ teaspoon of sea salt
- 1 tablespoon Worcestershire sauce
- ½ teaspoon dried tarragon
- 2 eggs, beaten
- ¼ cup ketchup

Method:

1. Place all the ingredients in a large bowl and mix well until combined.
2. Then shape the mixture into eight patties and refrigerate them for 10 minutes until firm.
3. Then switch on the air fryer, insert fryer basket, grease it with olive oil, then shut with its lid, set the fryer at 360 degrees F, and preheat for 10 minutes.
4. Open the fryer, add meatloaf slider in it in a single layer, spray with oil, close with its lid and cook for 10 minutes until nicely golden and thoroughly cooked, shaking the basket every 5 minutes and turning the sliders halfway through.
5. When air fryer beeps, open its lid, transfer sliders onto a serving plate, keep them warm and cook remaining sliders in the same manner.
6. Serve straight away.

Nutrition Value:

- Calories: 228 Cal
- Fat: 17 g
- Carbs: 6 g
- Protein: 13 g
- Fiber: 2 g

Pork Chops

Preparation time: 10 minutes
Cooking time: 28 minutes
Servings: 4

Ingredients:

- 4 pork chops, bone-in
- 1 teaspoon onion powder
- 1 teaspoon garlic powder
- 1/8 teaspoon allspice
- 1 teaspoon dried parsley
- 1 teaspoon paprika
- 2 cups crushed pork rinds

Method:

1. Switch on the air fryer, insert fryer basket, grease it with olive oil, then shut with its lid, set the fryer at 400 degrees F, and preheat for 10 minutes.
2. Meanwhile, prepare pork chops, and for this, brush them with olive oil on both sides until coated.
3. Place the remaining ingredients in a small bowl and then dredge pork chops in it until evenly coated.
4. Open the fryer, add pork chops in it, close with its lid and cook for 18 minutes until nicely golden and crispy, shaking the basket every 5 minutes, flipping the pork chops halfway through.
5. When air fryer beeps, open its lid, transfer pork chops onto a serving plate and serve.

Nutrition Value:

- Calories: 371 Cal
- Fat: 20 g
- Carbs: 1 g
- Protein: 44 g
- Fiber: 1 g

Rib Eye Steak

Preparation time: 10 minutes
Cooking time: 17 minutes
Servings: 1

Ingredients:

- 16 ounces rib-eye steak, about 1 ½-inch thick
- 1/2 teaspoon garlic powder
- 1 teaspoon salt
- 3/4 teaspoon ground black pepper
- 3/4 teaspoon steak seasoning

Method:

1. Switch on the air fryer, insert fryer basket, grease it with olive oil, then shut with its lid, set the fryer at 350 degrees F, and preheat for 5 minutes.
2. Meanwhile, stir together garlic powder, salt, black pepper, and steak seasoning and then sprinkle it on all sides of steak.
3. Open the fryer, add steak in it, spray with olive oil, close with its lid, and cook for 12 minutes until nicely golden and thoroughly cooked, turning and spraying with olive oil halfway through.
4. When air fryer beeps, open its lid, transfer steak onto a serving plate, cover it with foil, and let it rest for 10 minutes, then cut it into slices and serve.

Nutrition Value:

- Calories: 230 Cal
- Fat: 16 g
- Carbs: 0 g
- Protein: 21 g
- Fiber: 0 g

Chapter 9: Vegetarian

Yellow Squash

Preparation time: 5 minutes
Cooking time: 10 minutes
Servings: 4

Ingredients:

- 2 medium yellow squash, peeled, cored, ¾-inch sliced
- ¼ teaspoon salt
- 1/8 teaspoon ground black pepper
- 2 teaspoons olive oil

Method:

1. Switch on the air fryer, insert fryer basket, grease it with non-stick cooking oil spray, then shut with its lid, set the fryer at 400 degrees F, and preheat for 5 minutes.
2. Meanwhile, take a large bowl, place squash slices in it, add remaining ingredients and then toss until coated.
3. Open the fryer, arrange squash slices in the air fryer basket in a single layer, close with its lid and cook for 8 to 10 minutes until thoroughly cooked and golden brown, turning halfway.
4. Serve straight away.

Nutrition Value:

- Calories: 21 Cal
- Fat: 2.4 g
- Carbs: 0.2 g
- Protein: 0.2 g
- Fiber: 0.05 g

Stuffed Tomatoes

Preparation time: 5 minutes
Cooking time: 25 minutes
Servings: 4

Ingredients:

- 4 large tomatoes
- ¼ cup minced onion
- ½ pound ground chicken, extra-lean
- ¾ cup oats
- 1 teaspoon minced garlic
- 1 teaspoon salt and more as needed
- ¼ cup chopped basil
- ½ teaspoon ground black pepper
- 1 cup vegan shredded mozzarella cheese
- 1 tablespoon olive oil
- ¼ cup vegan grated parmesan cheese

Method:

1. Cut off the top of each tomato, remove its seeds and insides and then season with salt.
2. Take a plate, line it with paper towels, place tomatoes upside-down on it and let them rest until drained completely.
3. Meanwhile, prepare the filling and for this, take a large skillet pan, place it over medium-high heat, add oil and when hot, add onion and garlic and then cook for 2 minutes.
4. Add ground chicken and continue cooking it for 8 minutes until nicely browned and cooked.
5. Then remove the pan from heat, add oats, basil and both cheeses and stir until combined.
6. Switch on the air fryer, insert fryer basket, grease it with non-stick cooking oil spray, then shut with its lid, set the fryer at 350 degrees F, and preheat for 5 minutes.
7. Meanwhile, season tomatoes with black pepper and some more salt and then fill their cavity with the cooked chicken mixture until stuffed.
8. Open the fryer, arrange stuffed tomatoes in the air fryer basket in a single layer, spray oil on the food, close with its lid and cook for 10 minutes until thoroughly cooked and cheese have melted, turning halfway.
9. Serve straight away.

Nutrition Value:

- Calories: 180 Cal
- Fat: 7 g
- Carbs: 14 g
- Protein: 16 g
- Fiber: 4 g

Fried Zucchini and Yellow Squash

Preparation time: 20 minutes
Cooking time: 8 minutes
Servings: 8

Ingredients:

- 1 medium zucchini, sliced
- 2 cups coconut flour
- 1 medium yellow squash, sliced
- 1 teaspoon salt
- 2 cups oats
- 2 eggs
- 1 cup buttermilk

Method:

1. Take a large bowl, place zucchini and squash slices in it, pour in the milk and then let the vegetables soak for 15 minutes.
2. Take a shallow dish and place coconut flour in it.
3. Take a separate shallow dish, crack the eggs in it and then whisk until beaten.
4. Take a separate dish and then place oats in it.
5. When ready to cook, switch on the air fryer, insert fryer basket, grease it with non-stick cooking oil spray, then shut with its lid, set the fryer at 390 degrees F, and preheat for 5 minutes.
6. Meanwhile, working on one vegetable slice at a time, dredge in flour, dip into the egg and then dredge in oats until coated.
7. Open the fryer, arrange vegetable slices in the air fryer basket in a single layer, close with its lid and cook for 8 minutes until thoroughly cooked and crispy, turning halfway.
8. Serve straight away.

Nutrition Value:

- Calories: 334 Cal
- Fat: 4 g
- Carbs: 62 g
- Protein: 12 g
- Fiber: 4 g

Veggie Quesadillas

Preparation time: 10 minutes
Cooking time: 25 minutes
Servings: 4

Ingredients:

- 1 cup sliced red bell pepper
- 1 cup cooked black beans
- 1 cup sliced zucchini
- 1/4 teaspoon ground cumin
- 1 teaspoon lime zest
- 1 tablespoon lime juice
- 2 tablespoons chopped cilantro
- 1 cup shredded cheddar cheese
- 2 ounces Greek yogurt
- 1/2 cup drained pico de gallo
- 4 whole-wheat flour tortillas, each about 6-inch

Method:

1. Prepare quesadilla and for this, place tortilla wraps on working space, sprinkle 2 tablespoons of cheddar over half of each wrap, top cheese with ¼ cup each of black beans, zucchini, and red pepper, and then top with remaining cheese.
2. Cover filling with the other half of tortillas, making a moon-shaped quesadilla, then secure with a toothpick and spray with oil.
3. Switch on the air fryer, insert fryer basket, grease it with olive oil, then shut with its lid, set the fryer at 400 degrees F, and preheat for 5 minutes.
4. Open the fryer, add quesadilla in it in a single layer, close with its lid and cook for 10 minutes until nicely golden, crispy, and vegetables have softened, turning quesadilla halfway through.
5. When air fryer beeps, open its lid, transfer quesadilla onto a serving plate, keep it warm and cook remaining quesadilla in the same manner.
6. Serve straight away.

Nutrition Value:

- Calories: 291 Cal
- Fat: 8 g
- Carbs: 36 g
- Protein: 17 g
- Fiber: 8 g

Brussels Sprouts

Preparation time: 10 minutes
Cooking time: 14 minutes
Servings: 4

Ingredients:

- 2 cups Brussels sprouts, cut into quarters
- 1/4 teaspoon sea salt
- 1 tablespoon olive oil

Method:

1. Switch on the air fryer, insert fryer basket, grease it with olive oil, then shut with its lid, set the fryer at 375 degrees F, and preheat for 5 minutes.
2. Meanwhile, place Brussel sprouts in a large bowl, drizzle with oil, and then season with salt and toss until well coated.
3. Open the fryer, add sprouts in it, close with its lid and cook for 9 minutes until nicely golden and crispy, shaking the basket every 5 minutes.
4. When air fryer beeps, open its lid, transfer sprouts onto a serving plate, and serve.

Nutrition Value:

- Calories: 50 Cal
- Fat: 4 g
- Carbs: 4 g
- Protein: 1 g
- Fiber: 2 g

Spaghetti Squash Fritters

Preparation time: 10 minutes
Cooking time: 8 minutes
Servings: 4

Ingredients:

- 2 cups air-fried spaghetti squash
- ¼ cup coconut flour
- ½ teaspoon garlic powder
- 2 teaspoons sliced green onion
- 1 teaspoon dried parsley
- 1 egg
- 1 teaspoon olive oil

Method:

1. Switch on the air fryer, insert fryer basket, grease it with non-stick cooking oil spray, then shut with its lid, set the fryer at 400 degrees F, and preheat for 5 minutes.
2. Meanwhile, wrap air-fried spaghetti squash in a cheesecloth and then twist it well to remove excess water.
3. Take a large bowl, place spaghetti squash in it, add remaining ingredients, stir until combined and then shape the mixture into 4 evenly sized patties.
4. Open the fryer, arrange squash patties in the air fryer basket in a single layer, close with its lid and cook for 8 minutes until thoroughly cooked and golden brown, turning halfway.
5. Serve straight away.

Nutrition Value:

- Calories: 131 Cal
- Fat: 10.1 g
- Carbs: 5.1 g
- Protein: 3.8 g
- Fiber: 2 g

Artichoke Hearts

Preparation time: 5 minutes
Cooking time: 8 minutes
Servings: 4

Ingredients:

- 14 ounces canned artichoke hearts, quarter, drained
- 1/8 teaspoon garlic powder
- ¼ teaspoon salt
- 1/8 teaspoon ground black pepper
- ¼ teaspoon Italian seasoning
- 2 teaspoons vegan grated parmesan cheese
- 1 tablespoon olive oil

Method:

1. Switch on the air fryer, insert fryer basket, grease it with non-stick cooking oil spray, then shut with its lid, set the fryer at 390 degrees F, and preheat for 5 minutes.
2. Meanwhile, pat dry the artichoke hearts, place them in a large bowl, add remaining ingredients and then toss until coated.
3. Open the fryer, arrange artichoke hearts in the air fryer basket in a single layer, close with its lid and cook for 8 minutes until thoroughly cooked and golden brown, turning halfway.
4. Serve straight away.

Nutrition Value:

- Calories: 67 Cal
- Fat: 3.7 g
- Carbs: 6.6 g
- Protein: 2.6 g
- Fiber: 2.2 g

Roasted Rainbow Vegetables

Preparation time: 5 minutes
Cooking time: 25 minutes
Servings: 4

Ingredients:

- 1 medium red bell pepper, deseeded, 1-inch cubed
- 4 ounces mushrooms, halved
- 1 medium yellow summer squash, deseeded, 1-inch cubed
- 1/2 of sweet onion, peeled, cut into 1-inch wedges
- 1 medium zucchini, 1-inch cubed
- ½ teaspoon salt
- ½ teaspoon ground black pepper
- 1 tablespoon olive oil

Method:

1. Switch on the air fryer, insert fryer basket, grease it with olive oil, then shut with its lid, set the fryer at 350 degrees F, and preheat for 5 minutes.
2. Meanwhile, place all the ingredients in a large bowl and toss until well coated.
3. Open the fryer, add vegetables in it in an even layer, close with its lid and cook for 20 minutes until nicely golden and crispy, shaking the basket every 5 minutes, stirring halfway through.
4. When air fryer beeps, open its lid, transfer vegetables onto a serving plate and serve.

Nutrition Value:

- Calories: 69 Cal
- Fat: 3.8 g
- Carbs: 7.7 g
- Protein: 2.6 g
- Fiber: 2.3 g

Grilled Tomatoes

Preparation time: 5 minutes
Cooking time: 50 minutes
Servings: 2

Ingredients:

- 1 pound cherry tomatoes, halved height-wise

Method:

1. Switch on the air fryer, insert fryer basket, grease it with non-stick cooking oil spray, then shut with its lid, set the fryer at 240 degrees F, and preheat for 5 minutes.
2. Open the fryer, arrange tomato halves in the air fryer basket in a single layer, spray oil on the food, close with its lid and cook for 45 minutes until thoroughly cooked and half of their original size.
3. Then switch the temperature of air fryer to 390 degrees F and continue frying the tomatoes for 5 minutes.
4. Serve straight away.

Nutrition Value:

- Calories: 28.9 Cal
- Fat: 1.4 g
- Carbs: 2 g
- Protein: 0.4 g
- Fiber: 0.4 g

Buttermilk Fried Mushrooms

Preparation time: 20 minutes
Cooking time: 12 minutes
Servings: 2

Ingredients:

- 2 cups oyster mushrooms
- 1 teaspoon onion powder
- 1 teaspoon garlic powder
- 1 teaspoon salt
- 1 ½ cup coconut flour
- 1 teaspoon ground black pepper
- 1 teaspoon paprika
- 1 teaspoon ground cumin
- 1 cup buttermilk

Method:

1. Take a large bowl, place mushrooms in it, add milk, toss until coated and then let them marinate for 15 minutes.
2. When ready to cook, switch on the air fryer, insert fryer basket, grease it with non-stick cooking oil spray, then shut with its lid, set the fryer at 375 degrees F, and preheat for 5 minutes.
3. Meanwhile, take a large bowl, place flour in it, add all the spices and then stir until mixed.
4. Working on one mushroom at a time, remove it from buttermilk, dredge into the flour mixture, dip into the buttermilk and then dredge again into the flour mixture until coated.
5. Open the fryer, arrange mushrooms in the air fryer basket in a single layer, spray oil on the food, close with its lid and cook for 12 minutes until thoroughly cooked, turning halfway.
6. Serve straight away.

Nutrition Value:

- Calories: 355 Cal
- Fat: 9.7 g
- Carbs: 57 g
- Protein: 12.4 g
- Fiber: 3 g

Chapter 10: Fish and Seafood

Fish Sticks

Preparation time: 10 minutes
Cooking time: 25 minutes
Servings: 4

Ingredients:

- 1 pound cod fillets
- 1 1/2 cups pork rind panko
- 2 tablespoons Dijon mustard
- ½ teaspoon ground black pepper
- 2/3 teaspoon salt
- ¾ teaspoon Cajun seasoning
- 2 tablespoons water
- 1/4 cup mayonnaise

Method:

1. Prepare fish sticks and for this, pat dry cod fillets, then cut them into 1 by 2 inches wide sticks and set aside until required.
2. Place mayonnaise in a bowl, add water and mustard and whisk until combined.
3. Place pork rinds in a shallow dish, add Cajun seasoning, season with salt and black pepper and stir until mixed.
4. First, dip each fish stick into the mayonnaise mixture, then dredge with pork rind mixture, place it on a plate, and coat remaining fish sticks in the same manner.
5. Switch on the air fryer, insert fryer basket, grease it with olive oil, then shut with its lid, set the fryer at 400 degrees F, and preheat for 5 minutes.
6. Open the fryer, add fish sticks in it in a single layer, spray with olive oil, close with its lid and cook for 10 minutes until nicely golden and crispy, shaking the basket every 5 minutes and filling the fish sticks halfway through.
7. When air fryer beeps, open its lid, transfer fish sticks onto a serving plate, keep them warm and cook remaining fish sticks in the same manner.
8. Serve straight away.

Nutrition Value:

- Calories: 263 Cal
- Fat: 16 g
- Carbs: 1 g
- Protein: 26.4 g
- Fiber: 0.5 g

Cauliflower Rice with Shrimps

Preparation time: 10 minutes
Cooking time: 25 minutes
Servings: 2

Ingredients:

- ½ pound shrimps, peeled, deveined
- ¼ teaspoon salt
- 1/8 teaspoon ground black pepper

For the Rice:

- 24 ounces cauliflower rice
- ¼ cup chopped green onions
- 1 ½ tablespoon sesame oil
- ½ tablespoon soy sauce
- ¼ teaspoon salt
- ½ teaspoon ground black pepper

For the Eggs:

- 1 egg
- 1/8 teaspoon salt
- 1/8 teaspoon ground black pepper

Method:

1. Switch on the air fryer, insert fryer basket, line it with parchment sheet, grease it with non-stick cooking oil spray, then shut with its lid, set the fryer at 350 degrees F, and preheat for 5 minutes.
2. Meanwhile, take a large bowl, place shrimps in it, add salt and black pepper and then toss until coated.
3. Meanwhile, take a heatproof bowl, place cauliflower rice in it and then microwave for 5 minutes.
4. Drain the cauliflower rice, add remaining ingredients for the rice and then stir until mixed.
5. Spoon the prepared cauliflower rice into the fryer basket, close with its lid and cook for 15 minutes until thoroughly cooked, stirring halfway.
6. Then top the rice with shrimps and continue cooking for 5 minutes.
7. Meanwhile, crack the egg in a bowl, add salt and black pepper and then whisk until blended.
8. Pour the egg mixture into the cauliflower rice and shrimps mixture, toss until mixed and then continue cooking for 5 minutes.
9. Serve straight away.

Nutrition Value:

- Calories: 344 Cal
- Fat: 15 g
- Carbs: 29 g
- Protein: 23 g
- Fiber: 2 g

Pecan Crusted Halibut

Preparation time: 10 minutes
Cooking time: 8 minutes
Servings: 4

Ingredients:

- 4 fillets of halibut, skinless, each about 4 ounces
- ½ cup pecans, ground
- ½ cup corn starch
- ½ cup oats
- 3 tablespoons lemon pepper seasoning
- 2 egg whites
- ½ cup white wine

Method:

1. Switch on the air fryer, insert fryer basket, grease it with non-stick cooking oil spray, then shut with its lid, set the fryer at 375 degrees F, and preheat for 5 minutes.
2. Meanwhile, take a medium bowl, place the egg whites in it, and then whisk in cornstarch until blended.
3. Whisk in wine until well combined, and then whisk in 1 ½ tablespoon lemon pepper seasoning until smooth batter comes together.
4. Take a shallow dish and then place oats in it.
5. Working on one halibut fillet at a time, season it with salt and lemon pepper, dip into the prepared egg whites mixture and then dredge in pecan until coated.
6. Open the fryer, arrange halibut fillets in the air fryer basket in a single layer, spray oil on the food, close with its lid and cook for 10 minutes until thoroughly cooked and golden brown, turning halfway.
7. Serve straight away.

Nutrition Value:

- Calories: 432 Cal
- Fat: 16 g
- Carbs: 31 g
- Protein: 37 g
- Fiber: 3 g

Fish Skewers

Preparation time: 35 minutes
Cooking time: 8 minutes
Servings: 4

Ingredients:

- 2 fillets of salmon, 1-inch cubed
- 1 medium red bell pepper, cored, cubed
- 1 medium orange bell pepper, cored, cubed
- 1 medium green bell pepper, cored, cubed

For the Marinade:

- 2 teaspoons minced garlic
- 1 teaspoon salt
- 2 teaspoons dried thyme
- ½ teaspoon ground black pepper
- 2 teaspoons dried oregano
- 1 teaspoon ground cumin
- ½ cup olive oil
- ½ teaspoon ground coriander
- 2 tablespoons lemon juice

Method:

1. Take a small bowl, place all the ingredients for the marinade in it and then stir until combined.
2. Take a large plastic bag
3. pour the marinade mixture in it, and then add salmon pieces and vegetable pieces in it.
4. Seal the bag
5. turn it upside down until salmon and vegetable pieces are coated in marinate and then marinate in the refrigerator for a minimum of 30 minutes.
6. When ready to cook, switch on the air fryer, insert the fryer basket, grease it with non-stick cooking oil spray, then shut with its lid, set the fryer at 350 degrees F, and preheat for 5 minutes.
7. Meanwhile, thread salmon pieces and vegetable pieces into the wooden skewers.
8. Open the fryer, arrange skewers in the air fryer basket in a single layer, spray oil on the food, close with its lid and cook for 6 to 8 minutes until thoroughly cooked, turning halfway.
9. Serve straight away.

Nutrition Value:

- Calories: 255.4 Cal
- Fat: 6.2 g
- Carbs: 12 g
- Protein: 30.2 g
- Fiber: 2.8 g

Blackened Fish Lettuce Wrap

Preparation time: 5 minutes
Cooking time: 10 minutes
Servings: 4

Ingredients:

- 1 pound Mahi-Mahi fillets
- 2 ½ tablespoon Cajun seasoning
- 2 tablespoons olive oil

For Serving:

- 4 large lettuce leaves
- ½ cup mango salsa
- ½ cup shredded cabbage

Method:

1. Switch on the air fryer, insert fryer basket, grease it with non-stick cooking oil spray, then shut with its lid, set the fryer at 360 degrees F, and preheat for 5 minutes.
2. Meanwhile, prepare the fish and for this, brush the fillets with oil and then season with the Cajun seasoning until coated.
3. Open the fryer, arrange fillets in the air fryer basket, spray oil on the food, close with its lid and cook for 10 minutes until thoroughly cooked and golden brown, turning halfway.
4. When done, evenly divide Mahi-Mahi fillets among the lettuce leaves, top with mango salsa and cabbage and then serve.

Nutrition Value:

- Calories: 247 Cal
- Fat: 3 g
- Carbs: 32 g
- Protein: 25 g
- Fiber: 5 g

Catfish with Green Beans

Preparation time: 10 minutes
Cooking time: 25 minutes
Servings: 2

Ingredients:

- 2 catfish fillets, each about 6-ounces
- 12 ounces fresh green beans, trimmed
- 3/8 teaspoon salt, divided
- 1/4 teaspoon ground black pepper
- 1/2 teaspoon crushed red pepper
- 1 1/2 teaspoon chopped dill
- 1 teaspoon swerve sweetener
- 1/8 teaspoon coconut sugar
- 1/4 cup almond flour
- 1/3 cup panko breadcrumbs
- 2 tablespoons olive oil
- 1/2 teaspoon apple cider vinegar
- 1 egg, beaten
- 3/4 teaspoon dill pickle relish
- 2 tablespoons mayonnaise
- Lemon wedges for serving

Method:

1. Switch on the air fryer, insert fryer basket, grease it with olive oil, then shut with its lid, set the fryer at 400 degrees F, and preheat for 5 minutes.
2. Meanwhile, take a medium bowl, add green beans in it, drizzle with oil, season with 1/8 teaspoon salt, red pepper, and sweetener and toss until coated.
3. Open the fryer, add green beans in it, close with its lid and cook for 12 minutes until nicely golden brown and tender, shaking the basket every 5 minutes.
4. In the meantime, dredge fish fillets with almond flour, then dip in beaten egg and coat with panko bread crumbs, pressing them lightly into the fillets.
5. When air fryer beeps, open its lid, transfer green beans onto a serving plate, wrap with foil to keep them warm, and set aside until required.
6. Add prepared fillets into the fryer basket, spray them with olive oil, and continue cooking for 8 minutes until nicely golden brown and thoroughly cooked.
7. Prepare dip and for this, place mayonnaise in a bowl, add sugar, dill, vinegar, and relish and stir until mixed.
8. When done, season fillets with remaining salt and black pepper and serve with green beans, prepared dip and lemon wedges.

Nutrition Value:

- Calories: 416 Cal
- Fat: 18 g
- Carbs: 31 g
- Protein: 33 g
- Fiber: 12 g

Lemon Pepper Shrimp

Preparation time: 5 minutes
Cooking time: 8 minutes
Servings: 2

Ingredients:

- 12 ounces shrimp, peeled, deveined
- ¼ teaspoon garlic powder
- 1 teaspoon lemon pepper
- 1 lemon, juiced
- ¼ teaspoon paprika
- 1 tablespoon olive oil

Method:

1. Switch on the air fryer, insert fryer basket, grease it with non-stick cooking oil spray, then shut with its lid, set the fryer at 400 degrees F, and preheat for 5 minutes.
2. Meanwhile, take a large bowl, place all the ingredients in it and then stir until well combined.
3. Open the fryer, arrange shrimps in the air fryer basket in a single layer, close with its lid and cook for 6 to 8 minutes until thoroughly cooked, turning halfway.
4. Serve straight away.

Nutrition Value:

- Calories: 215 Cal
- Fat: 8.6 g
- Carbs: 12.6 g
- Protein: 28.6 g
- Fiber: 5.5 g

Tomato Basil Scallops

Preparation time: 10 minutes
Cooking time: 20 minutes
Servings: 2

Ingredients:

- 8 jumbo sea scallops
- 12 ounces frozen spinach, thawed, drained
- 1 tablespoon chopped basil
- 1 tablespoon tomato paste
- 1 teaspoon minced garlic
- 1/2 teaspoon salt and more as needed
- 1/2 teaspoon ground black pepper and more as needed
- 2 tablespoons olive oil
- 3/4 cup heavy whipping cream

Method:

1. Switch on the air fryer, then shut with its lid, set the fryer at 350 degrees F, and preheat for 10 minutes.
2. Meanwhile, take an air fryer baking pan and then line spinach evenly in the bottom.
3. Place scallops in a bowl, drizzle with oil, season with salt and black pepper, toss until coated, and then top them over spinach.
4. Place tomato paste in a bowl, add garlic, basil, ¼ teaspoon each of salt and black pepper, and cream, whisk until mixed and then spread the mixture over scallops.
5. Open the fryer, insert baking pan in it, close with its lid and cook for 10 minutes until thoroughly cooked and sauce is bubbling.
6. When air fryer beeps, open its lid, take out the baking pan, transfer spinach and scallops onto a serving plate and serve.

Nutrition Value:

- Calories: 359 Cal
- Fat: 33 g
- Carbs: 6 g
- Protein: 9 g
- Fiber: 2 g

Fish Cakes with Cilantro

Preparation time: 5 minutes
Cooking time: 10 minutes
Servings: 2

Ingredients:

- 2/3 cup oats
- 10 ounces chopped catfish
- ¼ teaspoon salt
- 2 tablespoons sweet chili sauce
- ¼ teaspoon ground black pepper
- 2 tablespoons vegan mayonnaise
- 3 tablespoons chopped cilantro
- 1 egg

Method:

1. Switch on the air fryer, insert fryer basket, grease it with non-stick cooking oil spray, then shut with its lid, set the fryer at 400 degrees F, and preheat for 5 minutes.
2. Meanwhile, take a large bowl, place all the ingredients in it, stir until combined and then shape the mixture into four evenly sized patties.
3. Open the fryer, arrange fish cakes in the air fryer basket in a single layer, spray oil on the food, close with its lid and cook for 10 minutes until thoroughly cooked and golden brown, turning halfway.
4. Serve straight away.

Nutrition Value:

- Calories: 399 Cal
- Fat: 15.5 g
- Carbs: 27.9 g
- Protein: 34.6 g
- Fiber: 2.8 g

Shrimp Scampi

Preparation time: 10 minutes
Cooking time: 7 minutes
Servings: 4

Ingredients:

- 25 shrimps, defrosted, peeled, deveined, cleaned
- 1 tablespoon minced garlic
- 1 teaspoon dried basil
- 2 teaspoons red pepper flakes
- 1 teaspoon dried chives
- 4 tablespoons unsalted butter
- 1 tablespoon lemon juice
- 2 tablespoons chicken stock

Method:

1. Switch on the air fryer, insert fryer baking pan, grease it with olive oil, then shut with its lid, set the fryer at 330 degrees F, and preheat for 5 minutes.
2. Open the fryer, add garlic, red pepper, and butter in it, close with its lid and cook for 2 minutes until the butter has melted.
3. Then add remaining ingredients into the baking pan, stir gently, shut the air fryer with lid and continue cooking for 5 minutes until shrimps have cooked through.
4. When air fryer beeps, open its lid, take out the baking pan and let shrimps rest for 1 minute.
5. Stir the shrimps, transfer them to a plate and serve.

Nutrition Value:

- Calories: 221 Cal
- Fat: 13 g
- Carbs: 1 g
- Protein: 23 g
- Fiber: 0 g

Chapter 11: Dessert

Key Lime Cupcakes

Preparation time: 20 minutes
Cooking time: 25 minutes
Servings: 6

Ingredients:

- 2 limes, juiced, zested
- 1 teaspoon vanilla extract, unsweetened
- ¼ cup swerve caster sugar
- 8 ounces Greek yogurt
- 2 eggs
- 1 egg yolk
- 7 ounces cream cheese, softened

Method:

1. Place yogurt in a bowl, add cream cheese and mix with a hand mixer until creamy.
2. Then whisk in eggs, egg yolk, lime juice, lime zest, and vanilla until incorporated and then evenly divide the mixture between six silicone muffin cups, reserving the rest of the batter for later use.
3. Switch on the air fryer, insert fryer basket, grease it with olive oil, then shut with its lid, set the fryer at 320 degrees F, and preheat for 5 minutes.
4. Open the fryer, stack muffin cups in it, close with its lid, cook for 10 minutes and then continue cooking for 10 minutes at 350 degrees F until thoroughly cooked.
5. When air fryer beeps, open its lid, transfer muffins to a wire rack, and let cool for 10 minutes.
6. Then place reserved batter in a piping bag, then pipe the batter onto the cupcake and refrigerate them for 4 hours until the top has set.
7. Serve straight away.

Nutrition Value:

- Calories: 218 Cal
- Fat: 14 g
- Carbs: 13 g
- Protein: 9 g
- Fiber: 0 g

Churros

Preparation time: 1 hour and 15 minutes
Cooking time: 35 minutes
Servings: 4

Ingredients:

- 1/3 cup unsalted butter
- 1 cup almond flour
- 1/2 cup coconut sugar
- 2 tablespoons erythritol sweetener
- 1/4 teaspoon salt
- 3/4 teaspoon ground cinnamon
- 1 teaspoon vanilla extract, unsweetened
- 2 eggs
- 1 cup of water

Method:

1. Cut butter into cubes, place it into a saucepan, then place it over medium-high heat, add salt, sweetener, and water and bring the mixture to boil.
2. Switch heat to medium-low level, add flour and stir it continuously until a smooth dough comes together.
3. Remove pan from heat, then transfer the dough to a bowl and let cool for 5 minutes.
4. Add eggs and vanilla, mix with an electric mixture until dough comes together, and then transfer the dough into a large piping bag with a star-shaped tip.
5. Take a baking sheet, grease it with olive oil, then pipe churros on it, about 4-inch long and cutting the ends with a scissor, and then refrigerate for 1 hour.
6. Then switch on the air fryer, insert fryer basket, grease it with olive oil, then shut with its lid, set the fryer at 375 degrees F, and preheat for 5 minutes.
7. Open the fryer, add churros in it in a single layer, ½-inch apart, spray with olive oil, close with its lid, and cook for 12 minutes until nicely golden, shaking the basket every 5 minutes.
8. Meanwhile, place coconut sugar in a large bowl, add cinnamon in it, stir until mixed and set aside until required.
9. When air fryer beeps, open its lid, transfer churros into the bowl containing cinnamon-sugar mixture, toss until coated, and cook remaining churros in the same manner.
10. Serve straight away.

Nutrition Value:

- Calories: 442.5 Cal
- Fat: 31 g
- Carbs: 33.2 g
- Protein: 9 g
- Fiber: 3.3 g

Fruit Crumble Mug Cakes

Preparation time: 5 minutes
Cooking time: 20 minutes
Servings: 4

Ingredients:

- 1 small peach, cored, diced
- 4 plums, pitted, diced
- 2 tablespoons oats
- 1 small apple, cored, diced
- 4 ounces almond flour
- 1 small pear, diced
- 2 tablespoons swerve caster sugar
- 1 ¾ tablespoon coconut sugar
- 1 tablespoon honey
- 2 ounces unsalted butter
- ¼ cup blueberries, diced

Method:

1. Switch on the air fryer, insert fryer basket, grease it with olive oil, then shut with its lid, set the fryer at 320 degrees F, and preheat for 5 minutes.
2. Meanwhile, take four heatproof mugs or ramekins, evenly fill them with fruits, and then cover with coconut sugar and honey.
3. Place flour in a bowl, add butter and caster sugar, then rub with fingers until the mixture resembled crumbs, then stir in oats and evenly spoon this mixture into prepared fruit mugs.
4. Open the fryer, place fruit mugs in it, close with its lid, cook for 10 minutes, then increase air fryer temperature to 390 degrees F and continue cooking for 5 minutes until the top have nicely browned and crunchy.
5. When air fryer beeps, open its lid, carefully take out the mugs and serve straight away.

Nutrition Value:

- Calories: 380 Cal
- Fat: 11 g
- Carbs: 68 g
- Protein: 5 g
- Fiber: 5 g

Grilled Pineapple

Preparation time: 10 minutes
Cooking time: 28 minutes
Servings: 4

Ingredients:

- 1 medium pineapple, peeled, cored
- 2 teaspoons ground cinnamon
- 1/2 cup coconut sugar
- 3 tablespoons melted unsalted butter

Method:

1. Switch on the air fryer, insert fryer basket, grease it with olive oil, then shut with its lid, set the fryer at 400 degrees F, and preheat for 10 minutes.
2. Meanwhile, place sugar in a bowl, add cinnamon, and stir until mixed.
3. Cut pineapple into spears, brush them generously with melted butter, and then coat them with the sugar-cinnamon mixture, pressing lightly.
4. Open the fryer, add pineapple in it in a single layer, close with its lid and cook for 10 minutes until nicely golden and crispy, shaking the basket every 5 minutes and brushing with melted butter halfway through.
5. When air fryer beeps, open its lid, transfer pineapple pieces onto a serving plate, keep them warm and cook remaining pineapple for 8 minutes.
6. Serve straight away.

Nutrition Value:

- Calories: 295 Cal
- Fat: 8 g
- Carbs: 57 g
- Protein: 1 g
- Fiber: 3 g

Banana Bread

Preparation time: 10 minutes
Cooking time: 45 minutes
Servings: 4

Ingredients:

- 3/4 cup whole wheat flour
- 3/4 cup mashed bananas
- 1/2 teaspoon salt
- 1 teaspoon cinnamon
- 2 tablespoons toasted walnuts, chopped
- 1/2 cup coconut sugar
- 1/4 teaspoon baking soda
- 1 teaspoon vanilla extract, unsweetened
- 2 tablespoons olive oil
- 1/3 cup Greek yogurt
- 2 eggs, beaten

Method:

1. Switch on the air fryer, insert fryer basket, then shut with its lid, set the fryer at 310 degrees F, and preheat for 10 minutes.
2. Meanwhile, take a 6-inch round cake pan, line it with parchment paper, spray with olive oil and set aside until required.
3. Place flour in a bowl, add salt, cinnamon, and baking soda and stir until mixed.
4. Crack eggs in another bowl, add mashed banana, coconut sugar, vanilla, yogurt, and oil and whisk well until incorporated.
5. Slowly whisk egg-banana mixture into the flour mixture until well combined, and smooth batter comes together, then spoon the batter into the prepared cake pan and top with walnuts.
6. Open the fryer, place cake pan in it, close with its lid, and cook for 30 to 35 minutes until top is nicely golden and the cake has thoroughly cooked.
7. When air fryer beeps, open its lid, take out the cake pan, then transfer cake to the wire rack and cool for 15 minutes.
8. Cut cake into slices and serve.

Nutrition Value:

- Calories: 180 Cal
- Fat: 6 g
- Carbs: 29 g
- Protein: 4 g
- Fiber: 2 g

Cheesecake Bites

Preparation time: 40 minutes
Cooking time: 12 minutes
Servings: 2

Ingredients:

- 1/2 cup almond flour
- 1/2 cup and 2 tablespoons erythritol sweetener
- 1/2 teaspoon vanilla extract, unsweetened
- 8 ounces cream cheese, softened
- 4 tablespoons heavy cream, divided

Method:

1. Place softened cream cheese in the bowl of a stand mixer, add 2 tablespoons of cream and ½ cup sweetener and mix until blended and smooth.
2. Take a baking sheet, line it with a baking sheet, place cream cheese mixture on it, spread evenly, and place it into the freezer for a minimum of 30 minutes until firm.
3. Then switch on the air fryer, insert fryer basket, grease it with olive oil, then shut with its lid, set the fryer at 300 degrees F, and preheat for 5 minutes.
4. Meanwhile, place almond flour in a shallow dish, add remaining sweetener and stir until mixed.
5. Cut frozen cheesecake into bite-size pieces, then dip into remaining heavy cream and dredge with almond flour mixture until well coated.
6. Open the fryer, add cheesecake bites in it in a single layer, close with its lid and cook for 2 minutes until nicely golden and crispy.
7. When air fryer beeps, open its lid, transfer cheesecake bites onto a serving plate and cook remaining cheese bites in the same manner.
8. Serve straight away.

Nutrition Value:

- Calories: 329.3 Cal
- Fat: 30.7 g
- Carbs: 6.6 g
- Protein: 6.6 g
- Fiber: 1.5 g

Apple Chips

Preparation time: 5 minutes
Cooking time: 15 minutes
Servings: 6

Ingredients:

- 6 large red apples
- 1/8 teaspoon ground cinnamon
- 1 teaspoon olive oil

Method:

1. Switch on the air fryer, insert fryer basket, grease it with olive oil, then shut with its lid, set the fryer at 350 degrees F, and preheat for 5 minutes.
2. Meanwhile, place core each apple, cut into wedges, then place them in a bowl, drizzle with oil and toss until coated.
3. Open the fryer, add apple wedges in it, close with its lid and cook for 10 minutes until nicely golden and crispy, shaking the basket every 5 minutes.
4. When air fryer beeps, open its lid, transfer apple chips onto a serving plate, sprinkle with cinnamon, and serve.

Nutrition Value:

- Calories: 608 Cal
- Fat: 6 g
- Carbs: 150 g
- Protein: 2 g
- Fiber: 26 g

Spiced Apples

Preparation time: 5 minutes
Cooking time: 12 minutes
Servings: 4

Ingredients:

- 4 small apples, cored, sliced
- 1 teaspoon apple pie spice
- 2 tablespoons coconut sugar
- 2 tablespoons coconut oil, melted
- 4 tablespoons whipped topping

Method:

1. Switch on the air fryer, insert baking basket, grease it with olive oil, then shut with its lid, set the fryer at 350 degrees F, and preheat for 5 minutes.
2. Meanwhile, place apple slices in a bowl, drizzle with oil, sprinkle with sugar and apple pie spice and toss until well coated.
3. Open the fryer, add apple pieces in the baking pan, close with its lid and cook for 12 minutes until tender, shaking the basket every 5 minutes.
4. When air fryer beeps, open its lid, take out the baking pan, transfer apple to a serving plate, top with whipped topping, and serve.

Nutrition Value:

- Calories: 233 Cal
- Fat: 10.6 g
- Carbs: 32.6 g
- Protein: 1.7 g
- Fiber: 3.6 g

Conclusion

Eating far too much fried food increases the risk of obesity and overweight. The more fried food you eat, the more likely you will be to develop diabetes. However, if you have meals cooked in Mediterranean refresh Air Fryer, the problem will not exist. So, it's time to turn to air fried food to decrease the fat intake and to lose some weight without reducing your fried food intake. Because air fryer helps to reduce the amount of fat.

www.ingramcontent.com/pod-product-compliance
Lightning Source LLC
Chambersburg PA
CBHW050635150426
42811CB00052B/842